# GROWING UP
# GENEROUS

## Engaging Youth in Giving and Serving

Eugene C. Roehlkepartain

Elanah Dalyah Naftali

Laura Musegades

*The Alban Institute*

Library of Congress Card Number 00-104852

ISBN 1-56699-238-9

# CONTENTS

Figures                                                                    v

Acknowledgments                                                          vii

Introduction                                                               1

Chapter 1.    NURTURING GENEROSITY AS A WAY OF LIFE                         7

Chapter 2.    THE UNEXPLORED WORLD OF YOUTH, MONEY,
              AND GIVING                                                   27

Chapter 3.    OBSTACLES TO ADDRESSING MONEY AND GIVING
              WITH YOUTH                                                   41

Chapter 4.    SERVING OTHERS: AN EMERGING EMPHASIS                         61

Chapter 5.    RETHINKING YOUTH GIVING AND SERVING                          79

Chapter 6.    CREATING A CULTURE OF GENEROSITY                            105

Chapter 7.    CULTIVATING THE PRACTICES OF GENEROSITY                     129

Postscript                                                               161

Appendix A.   RESOURCES ON YOUTH GIVING AND SERVING
              IN CONGREGATIONS                                            163

99955

Appendix B.  PROFILES OF HIGHLIGHTED CONGREGATIONS        175

Notes        181

# FIGURES

Figure 1.   NURTURING GENEROSITY IN A CONGREGATION:
            THE BIG PICTURE                                          24

Figure 2.   ORGANIZATIONS MOST LIKELY TO RECEIVE YOUNG
            PEOPLE'S CONTRIBUTIONS                                   28

Figure 3.   YOUTH WHO CONTRIBUTE TO CHARITY,
            BY RELIGIOUS AFFILIATION                                 36

Figure 4.   LEVELS OF YOUTH INVOLVEMENT IN SERVICE TO OTHERS         63

Figure 5.   HIGH SCHOOL SENIORS' TIME SPENT SERVING OTHERS           65

Figure 6.   BARRIERS TO YOUTH SERVICE INVOLVEMENT:
            YOUTH PERSPECTIVES                                       72

Figure 7.   SEARCH INSTITUTE'S DEVELOPMENTAL ASSETS                  84

Figure 8.   LINKING CARING TO SEARCH INSTITUTE'S FRAMEWORK OF
            DEVELOPMENTAL ASSETS                                     87

Figure 9.   EIGHT CULTURE SHIFTS: A TOOL FOR REFLECTION              91

Figure 10.  SUMMARY OF EIGHT KEYS TO NURTURING GENEROSITY           106

Figure 11.  THE PARR PROCESS FOR SERVICE-LEARNING                   138

No book—particularly none that involves extensive research—is a solitary task. We want to thank the many people who have played important roles in this process.

First and most important is to acknowledge that this book would not have been possible without the cooperation, time, and guidance of many people in congregations and other organizations across the country who participated in interviews, focus groups, and other activities. We especially thank the individuals we interviewed, whose insights are at the heart of this book.

- Joseph Bailey, senior pastor, Our Savior's Lutheran Church, Box Elder, Montana
- Thomas Bright, coordinator of justice ministries and Young Neighbors in Action, Center for Ministry Development, Naugatuck, Connecticut
- Dwight Burlingame, associate executive director, Center on Philanthropy, Indiana University, Indianapolis, Indiana
- Susan Butler, director of religious education, St. John's Cathedral, Albuquerque, New Mexico
- Walter Collier, consultant, Institute of Church Administration and Management, Atlanta, Georgia
- Jewell Dassance, director, Children and Family Development, Congress of National Black Churches, Washington, D.C.
- Jeffrey Dekro, president, the Shefa Fund, Wyndmoor, Pennsylvania
- Dara Duguay, executive director, Jump$tart Coalition for Personal Financial Literacy, Washington, D.C.
- Nathan Dungan, vice president, Stewardship and Brand Development, Lutheran Brotherhood, Minneapolis, Minnesota. Dungan developed

Lutheran Brotherhood's two workshops titled "Parents, Kids, and Money" and "Parents, Teens, and Money."

- Dennis Eisner, assistant dean, Hebrew Union College–Jewish Institute of Religion, Los Angeles, California
- Neal D. Gold, assistant rabbi, Anshei Emeth Memorial Congregation, New Brunswick, New Jersey
- Harriet Greenstein, youth director, Tifereth Israel Congregation, Columbus, Ohio
- Jules Gutin, assistant director, Department of Youth Activities, United Synagogue of Conservative Judaism, New York, New York
- Dean R. Hoge, professor of sociology, Catholic University of America, Washington, D.C.
- Rich Junghans, director of youth ministry, St. Michael's Catholic Church, Stillwater, Minnesota
- Mary Kohlsdorff, youth director, Ankeny Presbyterian Church, Ankeny, Iowa
- Adolphus Lacey, executive director, Ujamaa Community Development Corporation, Mount Vernon, New York
- Matthew York Lacy, youth pastor, Netarts Friends Congregation, Tillamook, Oregon
- Robert Leifert, executive director, Congregation Kehilath Jeshurun, New York, New York
- Nancy Levin, director, religious education, Kehilat Israel, Pacific Palisades, California
- Robert Wood Lynn, scholar in residence (retired), Bangor Theological Seminary, Bangor, Maine, and former senior vice president, Lilly Endowment, Indianapolis, Indiana
- Mary Nesbitt, pastor, Greater St. James Fire Baptized Holiness Church, Detroit, Michigan
- Donald Ng, senior pastor, First Chinese Baptist Church, San Francisco, California
- Arva Rice, Public Allies New York, New York, New York
- Paul Richard, executive vice president, National Center for Finance Education, San Diego, California
- John Ronsvalle, chief executive officer, and Sylvia Ronsvalle, executive vice president, empty tomb, inc., Champaign, Illinois
- Brandt Rosen, rabbi, Jewish Reconstructionist Congregation, Evanston, Illinois

- Thom Schultz, president, Group Publishing, Loveland, Colorado
- Wendy Schwartz, education and program director, Beth Jacob Congregation, Mendota Heights, Minnesota
- Mark Shapiro, rabbi, Sinai Temple, Springfield, Massachusetts
- Danny Siegel, chairman, Ziv Tzedakah Fund, Rockville, Maryland
- Cherie Smith, associate pastor for Christian education, Kirkwood Baptist Church, Kirkwood, Missouri
- Efrem Smith, youth pastor, Ginghamsburg United Methodist Church, Tipp City, Ohio
- Adam Stock Spilker, rabbi, Mount Zion Temple, St. Paul, Minnesota
- Heidi Tarshish, *na'aseh v'nishma* ("we will faithfully do") coordinator, Temple Israel, Minneapolis, Minnesota
- Mark Vincent, director, the Giving Project, Elkhart, Indiana
- LeRoy Wilke, director, Department of Youth Ministries, Lutheran Church–Missouri Synod, St. Louis, Missouri
- James P. Wind, president, Alban Institute, Bethesda, Maryland
- Robert Wuthnow, director, Center for the Study of American Religion, Princeton University, Princeton, New Jersey
- Alphonso Wyatt, vice president, Fund for the City of New York, and associate minister, Allen Temple African Methodist Episcopal Church, Jamaica, Queens, New York

In addition, several people helped guide us toward congregations to include in this research. They include Paula Beugen, Jewish Community Relations Council of Minnesota and the Dakotas, Minneapolis, Minnesota; Jewell Dassance, Congress of National Black Churches, Washington, D.C.; Naomi Eisenberger of the Ziv Tzedakah Fund, Millburn, New Jersey; Marsha Goldwasser, United Synagogue Youth, New York, New York; Dorothy Sharpe Johnson, African Methodist Episcopal Church Zion, Charlotte, North Carolina; Mike Jones, Reach Workcamps, Galeton, Colorado; Tom Klaus, Legacy Resource Group, Carlisle, Iowa; Bryan Perry, the Pittsburgh Project, Pittsburgh, Pennsylvania; and Slade Thompson, Gloria Dei Lutheran Church, St. Paul, Minnesota.

This book also grew out of a three-year project in Indiana called "Habits of the Heart: Strengthening Traditions of Giving and Serving among Youth." Led by the Indiana Humanities Council (IHC) and funded by Lilly Endowment, Inc., the initiative sought to address issues of philanthropy among young people through congregations and youth-serving organizations in

Indiana. Partners in the effort were Community Partnerships with Youth, the Indiana University Center on Philanthropy, and Search Institute. Special thanks to our colleagues at the Indiana Humanities Council who worked with us through this project, including Jerry Finn, Luana Nissan, Wynola Richards, and David Yates.

This book would not have been possible without the generous support of Lilly Endowment, Indianapolis, Indiana. Special thanks to Susan Wisely and Craig Dykstra, who invited Search Institute to join in the "Habits of the Heart" project, and who encouraged and guided the research in this book.

While three people take credit for this book as the primary authors, several other colleagues at Search Institute contributed to the process in significant ways. Thanks to Tom Berkas, now of Bethel College, St. Paul, Minnesota, who laid much of the groundwork for the research process and contributed significantly to shaping the ideas in this book. Thanks to Colette Illarde for diligence, perseverance, and patience in setting up telephone interviews. Thanks to Sandy Longfellow, supersleuth in tracking down resources, research, and other information. And, finally, thanks to Karolyn Josephson, for coordinating many details that made the writing process go well.

An important part of the process was inviting colleagues in the field and at Search Institute to respond to the manuscript. We thank the following reviewers, who offered helpful suggestions and guidance that have greatly strengthened the final product: Tom Berkas, Bethel College; James Conway, Conway Training Associates; Nathan Dungan, Lutheran Brotherhood; Dennis Eisner, Hebrew Union College–Jewish Institute of Religion; Marilyn Erickson, Search Institute; Jules Gutin, Department of Youth Activities, United Synagogue of Conservative Judaism; Kay Hong, Search Institute; Luana Nissan, independent consultant; Diana Mendley Rauner, Chapin Hall Center for Children; John Roberto, Center for Ministry Development; Janet Wakefield, Community Partnerships with Youth; and Susan Wisely, Lilly Endowment.

Finally, special thanks go to our friends and colleagues at the Alban Institute who encouraged us to write this book, then coaxed, guided, and encouraged us along the way. Particular thanks to Beth Ann Gaede, for encouragement, flexibility, patience, and guidance in the writing process. And to Jean Caffey Lyles, for careful editing that makes the book more readable and useful. It has been a pleasure to work with pros!

We're living in a society where money has more power than God; where human life is worth less than someone's jacket. We must teach our children about tolerance, unselfishness, and giving. We need to teach them that sometimes we need to compromise and give up something that would be good for us as an individual so that what we're choosing instead is good for all.

In the quotation above, a high school teacher in Michigan[1] sums up the challenge and opportunity of encouraging young people to give and serve. In a time when people of all ages make many choices based on "what's in it for me," young people need to be guided, motivated, and challenged to discover what they have to offer their communities, the nation, and the world—and then to be supported and affirmed in these efforts.

Where better to promote such a priority than in the faith community? People of all faiths share a commitment to acts of generosity. Furthermore, the religious community is at the center of considerable financial giving and service to others in the United States.

- In 1995, Americans gave an estimated $44.5 billion to religious institutions—far more than was given to any other type of charitable organization, according to estimates by empty tomb, inc., which tracks trends in religious giving.[2] Like adults, teenagers are much more likely to give money to a congregation than to any other institution.[3]
- The most common place for teenagers to start serving others as volunteers is through the congregation. And the more active young people are in their congregations, the more likely they are to serve others.[4]

Congregations clearly have tremendous opportunities to guide youth to give of themselves and their resources for others' benefit. And, indeed, the research on which this book is based suggests that a great deal of creative work is happening in churches and synagogues to encourage young people to give and serve. At the same time, important gaps persist between a commitment to generosity and an effective practice in congregations. Those gaps represent missed opportunities in a time when young people have much to offer, financially as well as through service to others. If congregations intentionally cultivate these generous habits early in life, they, their surrounding communities, and society will likely reap the rewards in lifelong commitments and involvement.

## ABOUT THE RESEARCH PROJECT

This book is based on a two-year exploratory project by Search Institute, a nonprofit research and education organization that specializes in the healthy development of children and adolescents. The project was part of "Habits of the Heart," an initiative led by the Indiana Humanities Council with the support of Lilly Endowment. The effort sought to gather and synthesize information from numerous sources to identify how congregations can more effectively engage young people in giving and serving. It included the following activities:

- Interviews with leaders in Jewish and Christian congregations that have exemplary or innovative approaches to engaging young people in financial giving and service (for a list of congregations, see appendix B)
- Interviews with national leaders and experts about issues, trends, challenges, and opportunities for encouraging young people to give and serve through congregations (for a list of these people, see the acknowledgments)
- Focus groups with young people in congregations about their experience in and perspectives on giving and serving (see appendix B)
- Examination of existing materials and research on youth giving and serving in congregations and related fields

These activities introduced us to information and ideas from disparate sources and perspectives. They included curricula and tools developed within specific faith traditions, research on service-learning and volunteering, financial challenges facing congregations, cultural attitudes about money, innovative models of youth work, similarities and differences between Jewish and Christian congregations, and the burgeoning industries seeking to tap into the extensive "youth market." These sources and perspectives offered a rich picture of what is happening with youth in this culture and in congregations. The research also suggested directions for the future, if congregations are to be more effective in engaging youth in giving and serving.

## WHAT'S IN THIS BOOK

This book uses the information we have gathered, first to create a mosaic of what is happening—and what could happen—in U.S. congregations to cultivate in young people a deep and lasting commitment to giving and serving. The first four chapters provide a context and rationale for a more vigorous and comprehensive approach to the issue of giving and serving among youth. We show how a wide range of factors has shaped the current state of youth giving and serving, including some of the differences across faith traditions. We examine the current scope of congregational efforts as well as the barriers to greater effectiveness.

The last three chapters suggest how congregations can be more focused and effective in encouraging young people to give and serve. From our perspective, this task involves more than "teaching." We propose that a true commitment to giving and serving requires exploring how all aspects of congregational life—from norms to relationships to activities to belief systems—shape young people's commitments.

## WHO CAN BENEFIT FROM THIS BOOK

While youth workers (ministers, sponsors, directors) play an important role in shaping young people's commitments toward giving and serving, many other leaders have important roles. Indeed, a serious challenge facing youth work in many congregations is that one or two professional or volunteer youth workers have sole responsibility for young people. Teenagers need the whole congregation to be a formative community for them.

This book recognizes and highlights the roles of the many people in a congregation who help shape young people's attitudes and commitments toward giving and serving. They include clergy (pastors, rabbis, priests), lay leaders responsible for stewardship or fund-raising, members of congregational service, missions, or social justice committees, and, of course, leaders in the youth and family programming.

Regardless of the reader's role or position in a congregation, this book will be most useful in the hands of an individual—a champion—with a passion and commitment to challenging congregations to address youth giving and serving in creative, comprehensive, and continuing ways.

## NOTES ON LANGUAGE

This book examines giving and serving in a broad range of Jewish and Christian traditions. This approach allows for rich perspectives and mutual learning. But finding language that communicates clearly in various traditions can be a challenge.

We have tried to use "generic" terms recognizable across traditions. We recognize that these substitutions do not capture all the intention and meaning embedded in the faith-specific language. But they do reduce the need to translate. Some of the common terms in this book (with some of their faith-specific counterparts) are:

- Giving—stewardship, *tzedakah* (acts of righteous giving)
- Service—*gemilut chassadim* (acts of loving-kindness), missions, social action
- Congregation—church, synagogue, temple, parish

We occasionally include faith-specific terms, within the context of material related to a tradition or to remind readers of the rich heritage and wisdom behind the vocabulary.

For the sake of flow, we have included only brief information in the text about the individuals we quote and the congregations we describe. Quotations from individuals that are not footnoted were drawn from 1999 phone interviews. More information on those interviewed is included in the acknowledgments, and on the congregations featured in appendix B.

## BEGINNING A CONVERSATION

When we began this project, we assumed that we would build on a solid foundation of existing information and resources. That is true with many congregations when it comes to serving. But we also discovered that congregations that systematically address financial giving with youth are rare, particularly in Christian traditions. Even rarer are congregations that do both.

As a result, we pulled together ideas and insights from many sources, creating a mosaic of possibilities for congregations. Rather than provide a definitive approach, this book is intended to prompt new conversations about how we engage young people. What do we expect from them? How can we involve them more effectively in giving and serving? What are the implications for all areas of congregational life? In the end, we hope congregations will respond with fresh, innovative approaches that inspire and cultivate generosity among youth—for today and for the future.

# CHAPTER 1

# Nurturing Generosity as a Way of Life

S ervice projects are the norm at Heritage Baptist Church in Cartersville, Georgia, and so are the high expectations that go along with them. The youth group has an ongoing relationship with a nearby shelter for children who have been removed from their homes and are awaiting placement. Eileen Campbell-Reed, minister of Christian education, works hard to instill in teenagers a sensitivity toward the needs of the children with whom they work.

The youth group engages with the shelter at least six to eight times a year. And Campbell-Reed encourages the deepening of relationships by having the youth include the children from the shelter at church events, such as holiday activities. "The emphasis is on developing relationships as part of service, not just going to the site once and doing a service project and never seeing the people again," she said.

•   •   •

The youth program at Beth El Synagogue, St. Louis Park, Minnesota, including service projects, is run entirely by the youth. The young people collect groceries for food pantries, rake leaves, and raise funds for the youth program and local charities. Young people set the goals, make the plans, and take the action together.

•   •   •

St. John of the Cross, a Roman Catholic parish in Middlebury, Connecticut, creates a range of service projects that teenagers and their parents can do together, depending on their level of interest and commitment. To get families interested, the parish invited families to take on simple tasks such as driving other families to the homeless shelter, cleaning and painting the shelter, or providing supplies that shelter guests could use. Some families organized the collection of these items during Advent. Eventually, six families made long-term commitments to make a meal for the shelter once a month.

●   ●   ●

Congregation Schaarai Zedek in Tampa, Florida, hosted a junior youth group event with the goal of acquainting its youth with the needs of those with physical or mental disabilities. In addition to learning from a variety of people with disabilities, the young people took part in a special Shabbat service that highlighted the importance of including everyone in the congregation's life. They also attended study sessions in which modern ethical dilemmas were explored in light of Jewish law.[1]

●   ●   ●

Like many other churches and synagogues across the country, these congregations have discovered the importance of focusing attention on helping young people become generous. This emphasis not only resonates with the tenets, priorities, and expectations of Christian and Jewish faith traditions; it can also lay a foundation for lifelong generosity through giving and serving.

In the past two decades, many congregations have made service to others an integral part of their work with youth. Most congregational youth programs include service projects, work trips, or social action. In contrast, relatively few congregations (particularly in Christian denominations) emphasize the ongoing practice of financial giving with youth. Furthermore, most congregational leaders are ambivalent about encouraging financial giving among young people.

Giving and serving are integrally related habits and disciplines that grow out of a sense of generosity, compassion, and concern for others. They can—and should—be important emphases for engaging young people in the life of faith. Furthermore, these two practices must be cultivated by a life-shaping community of faith, not just through a curriculum, an occasional project, or an isolated "youth program."

To set the stage, it's important first to share assumptions about the potential of youth giving and serving in congregations. What happens when a congregation strongly encourages giving and serving? How does this focus benefit the young people, the congregation, and the community?

## Why Link Giving and Serving?

In most congregations, giving and serving are separate activities. One committee (stewardship or *tzedakah*) focuses on financial giving. Another (acts of loving-kindness, outreach, missions, or *gemilut chasadim*) focuses on serving. The two often link up in youth work only when young people are asked to raise funds to support a service project or work trip.

In some ways it would be simpler to focus on one or the other. However, important connections between the two challenge us to build bridges between them.

### Conceptual Connections

Both giving and serving express similar internal commitments and impulses. Both reflect an "other-centeredness" and a sense of responsibility for and generosity toward others. Both are motivated by values of compassion, charity, and social justice. In short, giving and serving are two ways of tapping the resources of young people to respond to the needs of others. One focuses on sharing time and talent (serving), while the other focuses on sharing treasure or money (giving).

### Religious Connections

These two themes are often linked in the beliefs and practices of faith traditions. For example, Christians often connect giving and serving under the framework of "stewardship"—the responsible use of all resources entrusted to humanity and to individuals. Jewish traditions emphasize both giving and serving as obligations, or *mitzvot*. Some Jewish leaders also link *tzedakah* (giving) and *gemilut chasadim* (serving) under the umbrella term *tikkun olam* (repair of the world or social action).

Many traditions have clear links between giving and serving. For example, Mary J. Oates, Regis College economics professor, notes that "for two hundred years, American Catholics cherished as a religious value the essential link between gifts of money and gifts of voluntary service. For them, benevolence had to meet two criteria, one more important than the other. Unless accompanied by some form of personal service, however modest, the financial contributions, however large, cannot fully satisfy the mandate of religious charity."[2]

## PRACTICAL CONNECTIONS

People who give more are also likely to serve more. Research on both youth and adults suggests that commitments to giving and serving shape, influence, and reinforce each other. Independent Sector researchers report that young people who both contributed and volunteered (34 percent of all respondents) gave an average of 4.2 hours per week, compared to 2.7 hours for those who only volunteered.[3]

## THE RESPONSIBILITY TO GIVE AND SERVE

The Jewish and Christian traditions (as well as other faiths) emphasize compassion, generosity, service, and justice as priorities—even obligations.[4] Leaders in congregations, activists, and theologians can cite innumerable passages in biblical and other sacred and traditional texts that admonish the faithful both to give and to serve.

Despite this common heritage, the emphases, language, and practices of giving and serving vary widely across—and even within—specific faith traditions. The diversity of perspectives grows out of each tradition's interpretation of its scriptures and other sacred writings and also out of its theological accents, historical experiences, cultural heritage, and institutional structures. Here are brief, generalized sketches of how several major Judeo-Christian traditions approach giving and serving.[5]

## JUDAISM

In Jewish traditions, *tzedakah* (giving or, more literally, acts of justice) and *gemilut chasadim* (acts of loving-kindness or service to others) are considered *mitzvot*—divine commandments that Jews have an obligation to observe. Rabbi Rami M. Shapiro, founder of the Simply Jewish Fellowship, writes about *tzedakah*: "Tzedakah is a matter of justice and therefore a legislatable obligation. You are obligated to be generous to those in need whether or not you feel like it. One who does not give tzedakah to the needy is not simply uncharitable of heart, but in violation of the law."[6]

This sense of obligation has contributed to the place of giving and serving as integral themes in Jewish culture and identity. In addition, the Jewish people's long history of experiencing oppression, persecution, and displacement has reinforced the importance of caring for people who are marginalized in society. Indeed, as sociologists Mordechai Rimor and Gary A. Tobin write: "In the United States, a vast fund-raising network has been developed to assist in the support of Jewish organizations and institutions, individual Jews in need, and the state of Israel and other Jewish communities around the world. . . . Giving to both Jewish and non-Jewish philanthropies as a measure of Jewish identity reinforces the concept of tzedakah as an integral part of Jewish behavior."[7]

While Jewish traditions emphasize the importance of *tzedakah*, they also argue that *gemilut hasadim* (acts of loving-kindness) are even more valuable. According to the Talmud:

> Our Rabbis taught: In three respects is *gemilut hasadim* superior to *tzedakah*: *Tzedakah* can be done only with one's money, but *gemilut hasadim* can be done with one's person and one's money. *Tzedakah* can be given only to the poor, *gemilut hasadim* both to the rich and the poor. *Tzedakah* can be given to the living only, *gemilut hasadim* can be done both to the living and to the dead. (Sukkah 49b)

## MAINLINE PROTESTANT CHRISTIANITY

Mainline Protestant traditions (such as ecumenical Lutherans, Presbyterians, and Methodists) tend to emphasize acts of serving and giving as appropriate responses to God's grace, love, and generosity, rather than as an obligation or requirement. Religious historian James Hudnut-Beumler traces the Protestant ethic of giving to three theological understandings that emerged during the Protestant Reformation. He writes:

> First is Martin Luther's conception of giving as an *act of thanks* for God's unmerited grace. Second is John Calvin's view of the disposition of material resources as *stewardship* over something that is not ultimately of human ownership. Third is the Arminian/ Wesleyan understanding of giving as *volitional responses* to divine activity. These views about why one should give of one's resources continue to be blended and reblended into the reasons people say they give of their time and money.[8]

In addition to theological themes from the Reformation, the 20th-century emphasis on peace and justice in liberal Protestant churches was heavily influenced by the Social Gospel movement of the late 19th and early 20th century. This movement emphasized working to bring into reality "the kingdom of God on earth," a realm of peace and justice for all people. The focus led mainline churches to work actively for social and political change in society—civil rights for blacks, community development, nuclear disarmament—while also supporting efforts to meet people's basic physical needs (programs for battered women, migrant laborers, refugees, the homeless, and others marginalized in society).[9]

## EVANGELICAL CHRISTIANITY

Evangelical Protestants (such as Baptists, Pentecostals, and many independent churches) have responded to the biblical commands to "love your neighbor" and "give to the poor" differently at various times in history. Furthermore, evangelicalism contains a wide spectrum of perspectives on responsibilities to the poor, service and justice, and the faithful use of money. In his essay on philanthropy among evangelicals, sociologist Timothy T.

Clydesdale identifies four distinct traditions of giving and serving among evangelicals in America.[10]

The first strand—which Clydesdale labels "indifferent evangelists"—focuses on spiritual change or regeneration as the precondition of personal happiness. "To persons in this tradition," Clydesdale writes, "the ultimate need of all people was regeneration, for following regeneration would come certain happiness; all other needs were either unimportant or, at best, not of high priority."[11] This tradition is known for a lack of interest in—and even discouragement of—efforts to help the poor or to address social issues.

The second tradition, "dutiful stewards," emphasized duties, simplicity, and giving to the poor as outward signs of salvation. This perspective recognizes physical, economic, and spiritual needs, and emphasizes the importance of acts of charity for believers. It tends, however, not to address issues of social justice.

"Prophets of justice" is Clydesdale's term for the third tradition. It calls Christians not just to do acts of charity, but to "live a life of 'radical obedience' to Christ, speaking out and fighting injustice and oppression worldwide."[12]

The fourth tradition is what Clydesdale calls "professional care givers." This tradition grew up with the 20th-century expansion of evangelical involvement in higher education. These evangelicals seek to blend a concern for the spiritual with a broader understanding of poverty. The perspective is captured in a statement from the relief organization Compassion International: "Earlier in this century a debate over a 'social gospel' and a 'spiritual gospel' split the church. But we see no such dichotomy."[13]

## ROMAN CATHOLICISM

A commitment to giving and serving has been a hallmark of the Roman Catholic Church through the centuries, most visibly through the religious orders that have made charity and justice central to their ministries. John E. Tropman of the University of Michigan writes that "the central features of the Catholic ethic include orientations toward the community, toward family, toward the self-in-context. There is also a heavy emphasis on concern for others. . . . There is a tradition of 'share-ity' and a bias in favor of the poor."[14]

In the United States in the late 19th and early 20th centuries, Roman Catholics—many of them working-class immigrants—gave generously to support the building of thousands of churches and schools, and to support hospitals, orphanages, and other expressions of care. An emphasis on almsgiving to help the poor and suffering pervades the Catholic Church at the parish, diocese, and national levels, with some Catholic social-service organizations (such as Catholic Charities) being among the most widely respected charitable institutions in the country.[15]

In recent years, Catholic theology has placed a renewed emphasis on putting the needs of the poor and vulnerable first. "Our faith is profoundly social," the National Conference of Catholic Bishops has stated. "We cannot be called truly 'Catholic' unless we hear and heed the church's call to serve those in need and work for justice and peace. We cannot call ourselves followers of Jesus unless we take up his mission of bringing 'good news to the poor, liberty to captives, and new sight to the blind.'"[16]

In addition to a strong emphasis on justice, charity, and almsgiving, U.S. Catholics have also struggled in recent years to recover a notion of stewardship—which Bishop William E. McManus, a Roman Catholic educator, calls "an unpracticed tradition"—to support their churches. McManus notes that for centuries the main sources of support for the Catholic Church and its institutions were "taxes levied by governments with which the church was allied and income from rich benefices owned by the church or by wealthy individuals."[17] Through the history of the Catholic Church in the United States, a variety of other fund-raising approaches have been used, including pew rents (in the 19th century), fairs, dances, bingo nights, and church bazaars.

In 1992, the National Conference of Catholic Bishops approved a pastoral letter on stewardship, which addressed its many dimensions as a core element of Christian discipleship. The bishops called for "personal participation in and support of the Church's mission of proclaiming and teaching, serving and sanctifying."[18] This document grew out of discovery of alarming patterns in giving and serving among Catholics. According to Oates, American Catholics give financially at only about half the level of Protestants. This low level of monetary giving is accompanied, she reports, by "a serious decline in contributions of voluntary service." As a result, nearly a third of American dioceses are in financial difficulty.[19]

## AFRICAN-AMERICAN CHRISTIANITY

The patterns of giving and serving in African-American churches are heavily shaped by the experiences of slavery, segregation, racism, and widespread poverty. According to C. Eric Lincoln, who taught at Duke University, and Lawrence H. Mamiya of Vassar University, "Since economic values are both primary and predominant in American society, and are commonly used to determine social relations and social status, the most severe forms of racial discrimination against black people have been economic in character."[20]

Out of this history of oppression and economic marginalization has grown a strong sense of responsibility for caring for each other and meeting the needs of extended family, neighbors, and African-American institutions. Black churches have been a major conduit for this generosity, says foundation executive Emmett D. Carson: "Without doubt, the most important philanthropic institution within the black community has been, and continues to be, the black church. From slavery to the present, the black church has been an extremely versatile institution through which blacks could channel their philanthropic resources to respond to the changing social and economic conditions that threaten the survival of the black community."[21]

Many of the largest congregations have invested millions of dollars in community development and community institutions such as schools, nursing homes, credit unions, housing developments, and social-service agencies. Researchers Cheryl Hall-Russell and Robert H. Kasberg write: "Rather than being based on the principle of *noblesse oblige*, in which the rich assist the deserving poor through charitable acts, African-American giving and serving revolve around the notion of philanthropy as a communal enterprise in which the members of the community take care of one another."[22]

Sharing with one another is an integral part of African-American culture. As Hall-Russell and Kasberg concluded after numerous interviews and focus groups: "Most African-Americans do not consider their giving and serving remarkable. Extending assistance and offering support occur on a daily basis so consistently without fanfare that African-Americans view informal aid as merely natural, something a person does because 'it's the right thing to do.'"[23]

## The Faith Mandate

It is fairly evident, then, that giving and serving are consistent themes in the theology and teachings of Jewish and Christian traditions—even if these teachings are not consistently practiced. These themes surfaced also in our interviews with congregational leaders. Consider these statements:

- *"Tzedakah* actually doesn't just mean money. It's righteousness; it means doing the right thing. . . . We all come from the same place, and we are given a portion. If it is more than someone else, we are supposed to share it. You need to take care of yourself and your family, but that's not enough. Then you need to reach out into your community, and then into the world." (Heidi Tarshish, Temple Israel, Minneapolis, Minnesota)

- "We believe it is important to give and serve because this is the way that we please God. This is the way that we serve him: by giving to others, by sharing with others, by doing for others." (Mary Nesbit, Greater St. James Fire Baptized Holiness Church, Detroit, Michigan)

- "To be a Christian means that you have to serve. It's not like it's a choice. It's not an option. You give and you serve. It's a definition of being a Christian. So to help young people learn to understand what Christian vocation is all about should lead to them seeing how important it is." (Don Ng, First Chinese Baptist Church, San Francisco, California)

This emphasis on giving and serving across religious traditions is evident in the levels of giving and serving among American youth and adults. Many people of faith are quite generous with their time and money. They give away more of their income than the nonreligious. They are more likely to spend time serving others. Generosity is more likely to be part of their value system and lifestyle.

Yet it is also clear that these priorities are not consistently or fully practiced by the faithful. On the whole and across traditions, people of faith do not give or serve at the levels that might be suggested—or even mandated—by the traditions they follow.

## Why Now?

*Growing Up Generous* focuses specifically on nurturing generosity in young people during adolescence. The emphasis on youth is important for a number of reasons:

- The practices of giving and serving have their roots in childhood and adolescence. This reality is coupled with widespread concerns within the faith community and the philanthropic community about whether the traditions of generosity, giving, and serving are being adequately transmitted from one generation to the next.
- An expanding number of young people have considerable discretionary income, but they are not, by and large, being encouraged or taught to share it with others. Not only does this "giving gap" result in missed opportunities to address important needs in the short term, but it also raises critical questions about whether young people will develop their lifelong financial habits without thought to their responsibility to share with others.
- A growing emphasis, readiness, and interest in youth service and service-learning (which integrates service with intentional reflection and learning) in many settings—including schools, congregations, and youth organizations—provides an important opportunity to strengthen and expand service efforts.
- An increasing number of congregations (and other organizations) are recognizing that young people have a great deal to offer their congregations and communities, if they are only invited and equipped to do so.

A focus on giving and serving among young people could potentially address serious and pervasive challenges in today's culture (materialism, consumerism) while also tapping into teenagers' capacity and need to contribute to their congregation, community, and world. In the process, congregations can be strengthened in fulfilling their mission.

The priority placed on generosity within Jewish and Christian traditions could be the primary reason for emphasizing giving and serving by young people. However, there are five other areas of potential impact.

## PRACTICING THE FAITH

Serving and giving are concrete "practices" or disciplines that connect faith, life, and the world. Kenda Creasy Dean of Princeton Theological Seminary and United Methodist pastor Ron Foster suggest that "youth learn compassion by practicing acts of compassion. The hands-on experience of caring for others shapes our hearts to care for our neighbor out of love as well as obligation."[24]

This understanding of Christian practices resonates with Michael Lerner's interpretation of Jewish *mitzvot*, or obligations. He writes:

> When the Jewish story is told so that Jews really get it that we were given this incredible privilege of being able to witness in our own historical experience this possibility of transformation, and that the rituals and laws of Jewish life are ways of keeping that message alive and are embodiments of the best ways we can figure out for treating one another as created in the image of God, then we get a very different feeling about being commanded. . . . To be commanded in this sense is to have the dignity of being partners with God in world transformation and world healing.[25]

Congregations often emphasize engaging young people in service (or service-learning), in part because the concrete action appeals to young people and can have a transformative effect on them, individually and collectively. "At some point in time you have got to get beyond teaching and preaching to kids and have them actually explore what you have been teaching them," said the Rev. Efrem Smith of Ginghamsburg United Methodist Church in Tipp City, Ohio. "I think one of the best ways to do that is through giving and serving."

A growing body of evidence reinforces that perspective. For example, a 1998 Search Institute study of Jewish youth in Minneapolis found connections between service and Jewish identity. The study found that youth who volunteer are significantly more likely to:

- Be involved in Jewish-sponsored activities
- Be involved in Jewish-sponsored activities
- Be concerned about social justice and other Jewish causes
- Observe Jewish rituals

- Believe Judaism and a Jewish education are important and meaningful
- Emphasize maintaining Jewish identity[26]

It is not surprising, then, that many religious leaders find that engaging young people in service is also a powerful approach for nurturing faith. "What I have really discovered over my years working with youth," said Cherie Smith of Kirkwood (Missouri) Baptist Church, "is they will get the gospel better if they are doing the gospel. . . . My group will not sit around in a circle and do Bible study for very long. They'll do that for a while. But if you can get them involved doing the Gospel and then talking about why we're doing this and where it comes from in the text and what it says about who we are, they get that!"

Though there are important exceptions, most congregations have done little or nothing to connect financial giving to faith (though the connections are clear in tradition and Scripture). Indeed, Princeton University sociologist Robert Wuthnow contends that U.S. culture tends to see money as disconnected from faith. "Money has become the domain of financial advisors, bankers, investment brokers, and economists," he writes. "But religious teachings have always regarded money as a matter of the heart. . . . For many of us, compartmentalization is probably the most comfortable way of dealing with the relationship between our faith and our finances."[27] Discovering ways to link faith and giving, then, has the potential for enriching young people's faith journeys as they discover how it can shape all aspects of their lives, including how they earn, spend, save, and share their money.

## CONTRIBUTING TO HEALTHY DEVELOPMENT

In addition to the ways that serving and giving can strengthen faith, this focus can contribute to young people's overall well-being and development. The connections are strongest in connecting service to healthy development. Search Institute researcher Peter C. Scales says the research shows that service-learning contributes to youth development in three broad areas:

- Building prosocial values and, to some extent, prosocial behavior
- Enhancing aspects of personal identity, such as self-esteem
- Enhancing school success, such as grades and motivation in school[28]

Because the research is scant, it is more speculative to identify how financial giving contributes to healthy development. Clearly, sharing one's own financial resources with others reinforces and shapes social values and can deepen a sense of meaning, purpose, and contribution. A commitment to giving can set young people on a life course toward being contributing members of society who see it as their responsibility to look out for the well-being of others. And, finally, a focus on giving can help to shift priorities into balance in a culture where the drive to accumulate wealth can consume or overwhelm all other aspects of life.

The connections are clearer when we broaden the focus to include efforts to strengthen young people's financial literacy and skills. By helping young people become more competent and thoughtful in their money-management practices (including their giving), congregations not only help them avoid some of the all-too-common dangers of high debt and irresponsible spending, but also address many skills, values, and priorities.

The commitments to giving and serving are integrally connected to fundamental choices young people make about how they will use the time and money at their disposal. Such decision-making and priority-setting can have lasting implications for all areas of their lives.

## STRENGTHENING BONDS TO THE FAITH COMMUNITY

Jewish and Christian congregations share a widespread concern about how to keep young people actively engaged in congregations through middle school and high school and into adulthood. Search Institute surveys of public-school students in 213 communities show a steady decline in the percentage of youth who report spending at least an hour a week in activities in a religious institution. In sixth grade, 72 percent report that they spend at least an hour a week in activities in a religious institution. By 12th grade, that number has dropped to 54 percent.[29]

This decline in involvement and loyalty clearly has an impact on young people's giving and serving. If youth are not involved or connected, a congregation has little opportunity to nurture a commitment to giving and serving. However, recognizing young people as resources and engaging them in serving others has real potential for strengthening their bond to the congregation. Consider the following:

- A Gallup Youth Survey suggests that a key to keeping young people active in congregations may be to ask them to serve others. Of the youth surveyed, 20 percent said they were involved in activities sponsored by their congregation "to help less fortunate people." An additional 60 percent said they would like to be involved in this kind of activity.[30]
- Search Institute's 1990 study of mainline Protestant youth found that young people more involved in serving others were much more likely to say that their church meant a great deal to them. They were also more likely to say there was an "excellent chance" that they would be involved in church as adults.[31]
- A survey by the Center for Applied Research in the Apostolate (CARA) found that 63 percent of Catholic youth reported that the opportunities for service had attracted them to participate in their parish's youth program.[32]

Some leaders believe that engaging young people meaningfully in giving and serving may, in fact, be one of the best ways to keep them connected to their congregation. "My sense is that kids are overprogrammed in an unprecedented way," said Rabbi Brandt Rosen of the Jewish Reconstructionist Congregation in Evanston, Illinois. "And it's going to have to be more than getting together once a month for mere bowling. . . . If you're looking at competing in the marketplace of what kinds of things are vying for the attention of kids, what you can offer them—and they might not be able to get elsewhere—is social action."

## OPPORTUNITIES FOR MEANINGFUL CONTRIBUTION

Congregations and communities are strengthened through the gifts, energy, involvement, and talents that youth contribute. Furthermore, the desire to make a difference and to help others is a major motivator for young people to engage in service. Independent Sector asked teenagers why they volunteered. Here are their top three reasons (the percentages represent youth who say the reason is "very important"):[33]

- I feel compassion toward people in need.                45%
- I can do something for a cause that is important to me.   44%
- If I help others, then others will help me.             42%

Young people can also make a difference through their financial giving, yet this potential is largely untapped. Most congregations and denominations appear to be doing little to encourage young people to give a portion of their income to others, though if young people gave away a small portion of their gifts and earnings, that contribution could be a significant resource in addressing the world's human needs and injustices.

Young people often find a new level of commitment to giving and serving once they have done so. Danny Siegel, a prominent voice for youth involvement in service and justice, tells stories of young people who choose to contribute portions of their sometimes sizable bar or bat mitzvah gifts to others (usually by encouraging people who are invited to the celebration to contribute to a *tzedakah* fund, rather than giving gifts).[34]

## PLANTING SEEDS FOR LIFELONG COMMITMENTS

Encouraging young people to give and serve not only contributes to the community and world now; it also shapes the way young people contribute to society throughout their lives. Research suggests that people who volunteered as children or youth are more likely as adults to:

- Volunteer
- Be involved in their community
- Participate in political activities
- Have leadership positions in community organizations
- Believe they can make a difference[35]

Other evidence suggests that the same is true in the area of financial giving. Longtime givers to congregations or other causes often mention early experiences and expectations about giving that helped to establish lifelong commitments. For example, Thomas H. Jeavons, a philanthropy expert, writes:

Many of us will remember being in worship services with our parents and how important it was for us to put something in the plate (like mom and dad did) during the offering. While this may seem . . . a superficial imitation of behavior, children often quickly internalize the rationales for and attitudes behind such giving.[36]

Developing positive, lifelong habits is an important part of growing up. The things young people do shape their character, particularly when they have opportunities for intentional moral reflection. William Damon, director of Brown University's Center for the Study of Human Development, writes: "Young people must learn to act right habitually, as a matter of course. The moral life is built primarily on good habits."[37] He continues:

> In our study of people with high levels of moral commitment, we found that they eventually come to carry out their commitments in a spontaneous and nonreflective manner, as if by force of habit. There is a quality of "automatic pilot" that defines even their most courageous acts. . . . Such immersion is accompanied by feelings of great certainty and clarity of purpose. But it must be remembered that reflection played a key role in the initial formation of their strong—and eventually habitual—commitments.[38]

These positive habits or practices, then, begin forming early when youth have opportunities to combine concrete action with moral reflection. Intentionally providing these kinds of experiences can become the foundation for priorities and commitments that last a lifetime.

## HOW THE CONGREGATION SHAPES GENEROSITY

When one thinks of the notion of youth giving and serving in congregations, many concrete examples come to mind: service projects, fund-raisers, and encouragement to give financially. While these opportunities are an important part of the mix, they are not adequate, in themselves, to nurture a lasting commitment.

While such a commitment can be sparked or reinforced through a work trip or a special fund appeal, a lasting habit of giving and serving is shaped by many factors within a congregation, family, and community—not to mention the influence of the broader society and culture. Indeed, the values and commitments of generosity, caring, and responsibility for others are cultivated through a web of experiences and relationships across many years. The challenge for congregations is to identify how they can shape young people's experiences and relationships so that they are more likely to develop lifelong habits of generosity.

We have identified a framework of congregational factors, or keys, that nurture giving and serving among youth. Drawn together from disparate sources, the eight keys offer a mosaic of how a focus on youth giving and serving can help to shape congregational life (see figure 1). The eight keys (presented in depth in chapters 6 and 7) are:

## Figure 1

The eight keys for nurturing generosity in a congregation propose a congregationwide vision and approach to giving and serving with youth. The first four keys help create a culture of generosity. The last four keys focus on nurturing the practices of generosity.

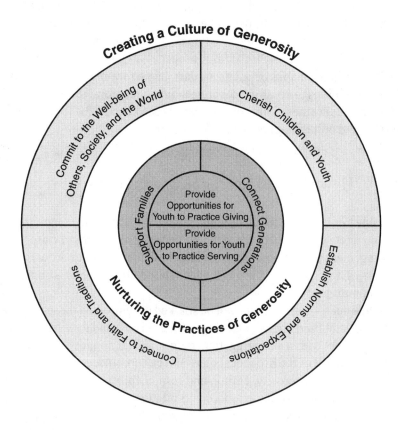

1. *Commit to the well-being of others.* This first key focuses on the importance of an articulated, faith-based vision and commitment to "the common good"—to the well-being of others, meeting needs in the world, and *tikkun olam* (repair of the world). This clear commitment is embodied in the examples set by leaders and the exposure of young people to social issues in light of their faith tradition.

2. *Cherish children and youth.* Children and youth learn to care for and value others when they are cared for and valued themselves. Congregations show young people that they are cherished by nurturing a warm and caring climate where they are invited to participate, serve, give, and lead; recognized for their contributions; and offered a comprehensive approach to engagement in congregational life.

3. *Connect to faith and traditions.* A general emphasis on nurturing faith recognizes that giving and serving by people of faith is a response of faith. Thus, young people need opportunities to learn the broad precepts of faith and apply them so that their faith shapes all aspects of their daily lives. A more specific emphasis ties serving and giving to the faith tradition. This dimension highlights the importance of holding up, teaching, and reflecting on the beliefs, practices, and expectations of giving and serving within the faith tradition and its rituals.

4. *Establish norms and expectations.* When people from congregations where giving and serving are strong are asked about their generosity, they sometimes have difficulty explaining. "It's just what we do," they'll say. "It's who we are. It's what's expected." In these congregations, a commitment to giving and serving has become the norm. Creating that kind of normative context begins with efforts to make giving and serving integral, ongoing emphases that permeate congregational life and that are continually reinforced.

5. *Provide opportunities for youth to practice giving.* Though essential, it's not enough to commit to the common good, cherish young people, connect to faith and tradition, and establish norms. These keys must be connected to concrete opportunities for young people to give financially within the context of a broader understanding about their responsibility as people of faith for how they earn, save, invest, and spend their money.

6. *Offer opportunities for youth to practice serving.* Young people need and want to serve through acts of compassion, justice, or charity. This engagement in service has the greatest impact (both for the youth and those being served) if it is thoughtfully planned, undertaken, reflected upon, and recognized.

7. *Support families.* Young people learn a great deal about giving, caring, and faith from their parents and in their homes. Congregations can have a much greater impact on teenagers' commitments by becoming partners with parents. Such a partnership requires integrating a family perspective into congregational activities, providing education, tools, and information to encourage giving and serving, and offering opportunities for families to serve together.

8. *Connect generations.* Young people discover the habits of giving and serving by seeing them lived out by many members of the congregation. Adult members must be guided and encouraged to recognize that their values and lifestyles influence young people—for better and for worse. In addition, intergenerational service activities provide wonderful opportunities to nurture relationships across all ages—relationships that become the vehicle for sharing values and commitments from one generation to the next.

## OPPORTUNITIES AND CHALLENGES

In the light of current realities, these eight keys offer opportunities and challenges to congregations. The opportunities lie in the rich heritage, languages, and practices of generosity that can be—and often are—integral to congregational life and youth work. And, given signs of growing interest in youth giving and serving, a new level of interest and openness may emerge to connect to congregations as resources. In the process, congregations have the opportunity to engage young people more actively and meaningfully.

The challenge lies in two complex realities. First, we live in a society that is, by and large, materialistic and consumer-oriented. Time and money are precious, to be protected, even hoarded. In this context, a commitment to a life of generosity is countercultural. The other challenge is that congregations have only begun to tap their potential for engaging young people effectively in serving and giving. Thus, congregations must engage in extensive self-reflection and re-examination of congregational programming, culture, climate, and systems to discern their areas of strength and how they can become communities where young people learn that being generous is a way of life.

# Chapter 2

# The Unexplored World of Youth, Money, and Giving

Money and materialism permeate American society in general and youth culture in particular. Through advertising, media, fashions, entertainment, and much more, consumerism dominates and shapes youth culture. The recent corporate interest in "reaching the youth market" is, of course, part of a larger cultural norm that affects everyone. Little wonder, then, that Robert Wuthnow argues that materialism is a social problem. "It is built into the fabric of society itself, pressuring us to conform to it, shaping our lives by virtue of the sheer fact that we cannot escape living in society any more than we can escape eating and sleeping."[1]

But although congregations tackle most other important issues in youth culture—from dating to sexuality to violence to family relationships—rarely do they talk about money with young people. And rarely do they raise the question of how youth earn and spend money or whether teenagers have a responsibility to share some of their wealth with their congregation, with people in need, or to address injustices.

Though reliable data on youth giving are scarce, available data suggest that relatively few young people give. Independent Sector research suggests that about two out of five young people ages 12 to 17 (41 percent) made a charitable contribution in the past year. When they give, they are most likely to give to a religious organization, as shown in figure 2 on the following page.

## Figure 2

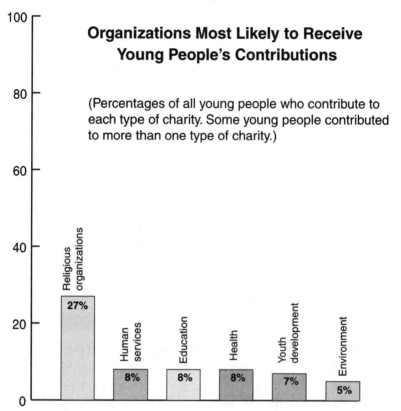

**Organizations Most Likely to Receive Young People's Contributions**

(Percentages of all young people who contribute to each type of charity. Some young people contributed to more than one type of charity.)

SOURCE: Virginia A. Hodgkinson and Murray S. Weitzman, *Volunteering and Giving among Teenagers 12 to 17 Years of Age: Findings from a National Survey. 1996 Edition* (Washington, DC: Independent Sector, 1997), 18.

Young people are less likely to give than adults, and to give slightly lower percentages of their income. According to Independent Sector, 70 percent of adults and 41 percent of youth made charitable contributions in 1996. Adult givers contributed, on average, 2.1 percent of their income to charitable causes, including their congregation. We estimate that, on average, teenage contributors give about 1.8 percent of income.[2]

The relatively low levels of youth giving reflect a broader issue: young people get far too little positive, values-based guidance about money and finances anywhere in their lives. In *An Asset Builder's Guide to Youth and Money*, writer and parent educator Jolene L. Roehlkepartain summarizes the situation:

> Outside of some economics classes and some family settings, there are few opportunities for young people to explore and study personal finances with the help of adults who care about them and are concerned about their well-being. If you ask adults who work with youth why this is so, they cite their own discomfort with financial matters, the belief that teaching about money is the responsibility of the family, and a fear that the topic is difficult to deal with in groups of young people from disparate economic situations.
>
> The irony is that most of us don't give a second thought to billboards, magazines, television, movies, and all the other impersonal tools used to "teach" young people about how to use their money. By not dealing directly with money issues in places like schools, congregations, and youth-serving organizations—places that are focused on nurturing young people—we surrender this opportunity to those who are focused on selling to them.[3]

In most general books on giving or fund-raising in congregations,[4] the reader is hard-pressed to find much information, if any, about teenagers as contributors—and no wonder. Researchers consistently find that giving is closely tied to age. Young adults also give very little compared to older adults.[5]

So is focusing on youth a waste of energy? From a short-term, bottom-line perspective, that may be true. But "short term" and "bottom line" don't get us far in matters of faith shaping and habit forming. Indeed, much more is at stake for today's adolescents when it comes to money and giving than how to pay the bills or which charities to support. What's at stake are critical questions about what they value and are committed to; whether their financial choices will be guided primarily by the consumerist and individualistic forces that dominate the U.S. economy and culture. Can congregations counterbalance those influences by holding up the values of generosity, justice, and communal responsibility that are integral to Judeo-Christian traditions?

This chapter places the issue of youth giving in several contexts. First, we look at the broad issues of youth and money and efforts to educate youth about money. Then we explore the extent to which congregations address youth giving. We conclude by highlighting barriers to such a focus in congregations as well as opportunities to address the issue in fresh, engaging ways.

## "Consumers with a Mission"

Madison Avenue, Hollywood, Wall Street, and other economic power centers have discovered "the youth market." They know that money habits formed early help to set the spending patterns for a lifetime. And they have found that many young people have money. According to Peter Zollo, president of Teenage Research Unlimited (TRU):

- The 31.1 million young people (ages 12 to 19) in the United States spent about $153 billion in 1999 ($105 billion of their own income from jobs, allowance, and gifts). Each week, teen females spent, on average, $60 of their own money; teen males spent $55.[6] Spending increases significantly through adolescence. In 1998 total spending was $53 per week for 12- to 15-year-olds, but it doubled to $103 per week for 16- to 17-year-olds.
- Teenagers spend, on average, 3.1 hours in shopping malls a week. (The same young people reported spending, on average, 2.6 hours "going to religious functions" and 1.2 hours "doing volunteer work.")
- Three out of five young people get money from a full- or part-time job. In addition, just over half (52 percent) said they get money "as needed" from their parents.
- "Having enough money" is the No. 2 concern for teenagers, with 48 percent saying it was a big worry.[7]

"Kid buying power is increasing," writes youth market expert Dan S. Acuff. The result, he contends, is that young people have much more direct family purchasing power and influence "when it comes to which restaurants and fast-food outlets to frequent, which pizza to order, which groceries and home necessities to buy, which computer systems, which brands of clothing—even which type of automobile to buy for the family."[8]

Advertisers, marketers, and retailers spend millions of dollars trying to tap into the youth market. A wide array of conferences, newsletters, books, and consultants now address the youth market. "Children are being targeted as marketing objects [as] never before," said Paul Richard, executive vice president of the National Center for Finance Education in San Diego.

The teens-as-consumers mentality gives pause to people of faith for a number of reasons. One is its emphasis on those who have significant sums of discretionary money at their disposal. It ignores the reality that about one in five young people under age 18 lives below the poverty line ($16,035 per year for a family of four).[9]

Young people who live in poverty—and those who live within modest means—are not insulated from the advertising push. They feel tremendous pressure from peers and the media to spend far beyond their means—pressure that can lead them to make careless or dangerous choices.

Another reason the youth marketing world gives pause is that its tone, language, and assumptions can be alien, even disturbing, to many people of faith. Consider this bold—and disturbing—call to action from Peter Zollo, president of Teenage Research Unlimited: "Teen spending is on the rise, and few teens are saddled with the payments that inhibit adult spending, like rent, utilities, and groceries. Teens' considerable income is almost exclusively discretionary. They are consumers with a mission: they want to spend on whatever happens to please them. What a compelling advertising target!"[10]

This advertising and the media have a powerful influence on how young people understand themselves and their money. Paul Richard warned: "Young people are becoming increasingly the target of marketing programs. They are becoming the targets of products and services that have been specifically developed for them. So it is critical that young people . . . learn what they are being confronted with every day in terms of the messages to spend."

While other voices seek to balance the spend-all-you-can messages, those perspectives are much less pervasive and consistent in this culture—a disparity posing an important challenge to the faith community. Robert

Wuthnow suggested: "Both parents and kids are bombarded by messages from advertising on television and in the newspapers, and now on the Internet, to buy more things and maybe even work harder and save more to get those things. . . . You need kind of a supportive counterculture to give different values from the ones we get from the mass media and in the workplace." It is also important to place young people's wealth, spending, and consumerism within the overall context of a society and faith communities that are, by many standards, wealthy. "We are a rich society," said Jeffrey Dekro of the Shefa Fund. "We may be a ridiculously rich society, and there may be a tremendous need for a social critique."

Nathan Dungan of Lutheran Brotherhood added that the power of the consumption-driven economy places "enormous pressure to live in a state of hypnotic consumption." He noted how easy it is to form bad habits that trap people in cycles of debt, stress, and overconsumption.

## Encouraging Financial Responsibility

While the world of marketing has focused exclusively on encouraging young people to spend their money as they please, a growing movement (particularly in schools) seeks to balance those messages with a sense of financial responsibility. These efforts focus on helping young people develop a range of financial skills, including money management, saving, investing, and responsible spending.

Organizations and coalitions promote "financial literacy" and "economic literacy" among young people as well as adults.[11] Several youth-serving organizations (such as Girl Scouts of the USA, Girls Inc., and the Cooperative Extension Service) have focused attention on strengthening young people's financial and economic knowledge and skills. Banks, investment companies, and other financial service organizations are creating Web sites, financial services, and educational materials designed specifically for the young.

These financial literacy efforts could be important resources for helping young people develop more responsible money-management skills, including developing and sticking to a budget, using credit cards responsibly, dealing with debt, being a smart consumer, and investing in responsible ways. Such learning can also help to address many of the excesses and imbalances communicated through the market-driven focus of the media and advertising.

## GIVING: THE GAP IN FINANCIAL EDUCATION

As valuable as financial education can be, most such efforts focus primarily on how to manage, spend, and save money. Rarely does charity, philanthropic giving, or religious giving receive more than cursory mention. Everyone with whom we spoke in the financial literacy field agreed that sharing or giving away money is part of responsible money management. However, the materials we reviewed tell a different story.

For example, the Jump$tart Coalition for Personal Financial Literacy has developed a series of 114 benchmarks of what young people should know by the time they graduate from high school.[12] The coalition also surveyed high school seniors in light of these benchmarks. Yet nowhere is the issue of philanthropic or charitable giving mentioned. Similarly, the coalition's Web site includes an extensive database of more than 250 educational resources on financial literacy for children and youth. In summer 2000, the standard key words for categorizing resources included no mention of philanthropic or charitable giving. Furthermore, a search of the database using key words such as charity, giving, or philanthropy revealed only one resource (which was written for parents).

The Jump$tart Coalition is not unique, but an example of a larger pattern. The High School Financial Planning Program from the National Endowment for Financial Education and the Cooperative Extension Service does not discuss giving in its extensive (and helpful) information on everything from salary to insurance to debt to investments.[13] A survey titled *Youth and Money 1999* from the American Savings Education Council asks students about their financial knowledge and practices but does not ask about giving.[14]

There are some exceptions. Girls, Inc., launched a financial literacy initiative for girls that includes a clear focus on giving.[15] Similarly, material from Lutheran Brotherhood to help parents and children learn financial skills emphasizes giving, or sharing (growing, in part, out of the financial service organization's faith base).[16] And a short money-management guide for teachers and students from Merrill Lynch and the U.S. Fund for UNICEF includes information on "sharing our money."[17] A few money-management books for parents and teenagers include short sections on giving.[18]

But these exceptions are far outweighed by the vast majority of resources that ignore giving as an integral part of responsible financial management—not only for people of faith but for a society that depends on a philanthropic or nonprofit sector to provide for the common good. Where are young people being invited—even encouraged—to challenge the priorities and messages of a consumerist, buy-it-if-you-can culture? Where will young people be encouraged to take alternative paths?

These questions about values, worldview, priorities, and identity are the kinds of issues with which people of faith have struggled for centuries. Yet such questions are too often ignored, neglected, or avoided in the faith community when it comes to money. Robert Wuthnow writes:

> In our own society, most of us have been taught to think of money in purely secular terms. Reading *Money* magazine, paging through the *Wall Street Journal* or taking a course in economics, we gain the impression that money is simply a medium of exchange. We are taught that money is best understood by economists, not by priests, that we should be rational about it, not superstitious, and that how we spend it should be determined by our desires and preferences. . . . If we think about our own views of money, though, we know that it is much more than economists lead us to believe. It has meaning. And it is thus connected with our beliefs and values—whether we admit it or not.[19]

All religious traditions have a lot to say about money, wealth, lifestyle, and our responsibilities to each other. But how well are those traditions shaping the lives of the faithful? And how well are they being mined for guidance for young people living in a culture of excessive materialism?

Examining congregational youth work reveals divergent answers. A few congregations seem to be effective in weaving a commitment to giving into everything they do. In most, however, financial giving is rarely addressed directly with young people.

## STRONG TRADITIONS OF GIVING

In some congregations, the responsibility to give financially is deeply embedded in the life of the congregation and in its understanding of faith. That commitment is passed on to young people in both systematic and informal ways as part of the underlying culture of the congregation. In general terms, the emphasis on giving tends to be stronger in more conservative religious traditions and in congregations that are part of minority faith traditions and cultural groups (such as Judaism and African-American churches).

One subset of the religious community that generally contributes at higher levels is made up of those who are more conservative and who have higher levels of religious observance and participation. For example, surveys comparing giving across denominations have found that Latter-day Saints, Adventists, Assemblies of God, and Church of God members give most generously, based on the percentage of income given.[20] By some estimates, evangelical Christians give twice as much as mainline Protestants and almost three times as much as Roman Catholics.[21]

Comparisons of giving in Jewish movements find similar patterns. The 1990 Council of Jewish Federations National Jewish Population Study found that 83 percent of Jewish adults who affiliate with the Orthodox movement contributed to Jewish philanthropic causes, compared to 71 percent of Conservative Jews and 61 percent of Reform Jews.[22]

There is also evidence that congregations that are part of minority faith traditions or cultures within the United States (including Jewish synagogues and temples, and churches serving people of color) are more likely to emphasize giving. Indeed, Independent Sector research on youth giving indicates, for example, somewhat lower levels of giving among Christian youth than youth from other faith traditions (which include Jews, Muslims, Mormons, and others). (See figure 3 on the following page.)

This emphasis on giving may be driven by the constant challenge to come up with resources to meet needs within the community. For example, in the wake of slavery, Jim Crow laws, and segregation, African-American churches became the hub of community life. As Lawrence N. Jones of Howard University School of Divinity has observed, "As the only institution which has proven itself viable and continues to be under the control of its members, black churches have had to assume welfare roles to a degree much greater than typically required of white congregations."[23]

Foundation executive Emmett D. Carson notes that levels of giving by African Americans to their churches is similar to the levels among white churchgoers (as a percentage of personal income); however, black churches tend to distribute more of the contributions into the community. "Blacks continue their tradition of using their churches as an important conduit for the distribution of money to individuals and organizations in need of financial support," he writes. "While similar percentages of blacks and whites make the same level of contribution to their respective churches, blacks were

# Figure 3

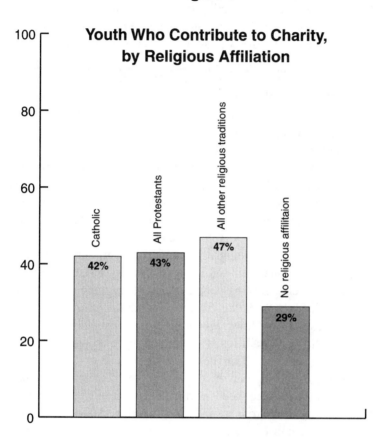

Youth Who Contribute to Charity, by Religious Affiliation

SOURCE: Virginia A. Hodgkinson and Murray S. Weitzman, *Volunteering and Giving among Teenagers 12 to 17 Years of Age: Findings from a National Survey. 1996 Edition* (Washington, DC: Independent Sector, 1997), 21.

found to be more active than whites in using church contributions to support individuals and organizations."[24]

In the Jewish community, the commitment to giving (*tzedakah*) is deeply embedded in the rituals and obligations or *mitzvot* of faith. The ongoing need for financial support has reinforced the priority. Says Jeffrey Dekro of the Shefa Fund: "Overall, the Jewish community experiences itself constantly as . . . being in a position where it needs to come up with resources in response to this problem or that problem." In the latter half of the 20th century, for example, a great deal of Jewish giving focused on critical issues for the Jewish community—supporting Jewish institutions, the state of Israel, and Jews facing persecution around the world.[25]

There are reasons, however, to fear that these historic strengths may be at risk. A key issue is a potential gap between expectations and realities. For example, despite the clear understanding among Jewish leaders that significant giving is an obligation, or *mitzvah*, many Jews do not live up to the expectations of their faith. A study by the United Jewish Federation of MetroWest in New Jersey found that only about three-fourths of Jewish adults give money to either Jewish or non-Jewish philanthropies. And 64 percent of those who gave contributed less than $100 per year.[26]

According to Anita H. Plotinsky of the Association for Research on Nonprofit Organizations and Voluntary Action, "Among fundraising professionals, it is widely believed that Jews are generous and that American Jewish philanthropy is spectacularly successful. The fact is, however, that giving has declined sharply in the mainstream Jewish community as assimilation and secularism have climbed. . . . Giving does remain strong among observant Jews, who constitute a small but growing segment of the American Jewish population."[27]

Similar concerns have been expressed about giving to African-American churches. Authors of the study of giving in black churches noted that "concern has been expressed by African-American clergy and laity across the country about the ability of Black churches to actually minister to the rising social, economic and moral needs of African-American communities, and whether current levels of giving to the church are adequate to meet the expense of outreach ministries." Researchers note several factors that contribute to the strain, including demographic changes in African-American households and "the neutral-to-negative attitudes of many younger African-Americans towards the church."[28]

There are also reasons not to be sanguine among Christian conservatives. John and Sylvia Ronsvalle note that, while higher than in mainline

Christian denominations, per capita giving among evangelicals is declining. Furthermore, a greater proportion of members' gifts is being used to support programs and activities within their own congregation, with less going to benevolent causes.[29]

Finally, it is also important to note that the information on giving among religious conservatives and among cultural and religious minorities is based largely on adult giving patterns, not on youth giving or on how assiduously congregations nurture commitments to give among the young. If the rich histories of giving are not passed on to the younger generations, they may be weakened—just as expectations have weakened in traditions such as Roman Catholicism and mainline Protestantism.

## A WIDESPREAD SILENCE IN CONGREGATIONS

Some congregations and traditions seem to be effective in cultivating in young people a commitment to giving. However, few congregations actively help young people integrate their faith priorities with their financial choices, helping them develop a consistent commitment to share their financial resources with others.

When we began research for this book, we asked people in a wide range of organizations and denominations to nominate Christian churches that were doing innovative things to encourage young people's financial giving. We found many congregations that are actively engaging youth in service to others. However, after contacting more than 100 Christian congregations nationwide, we found no Christian church that was assertively or innovatively encouraging youth to give financially. (Some included youth in congregationwide stewardship efforts or touched on giving as part of confirmation, but nothing more than that.)

Most people we talked with in congregations, denominations, and other Christian organizations had not really thought about whether and how to address financial giving among young people. Said one denominational leader: "Very honestly, I don't see a lot of emphasis on [giving]." He noted, for example, that the topic is rarely on the agenda at regional or national youth events. Indeed, most Christian denominational youth departments do not address stewardship at all, leaving the topic to the stewardship department, which rarely considers youth to be one of its constituencies. In addition, an examination of prominent Web sites for Christian youth ministry found no mention of stewardship or giving.

The silence noted at the national level seems to be replicated at the congregational level. Focus groups with youth workers in Christian congregations found that many hadn't even thought about the topic. Several were uncomfortable that it had been brought up. If the topic is addressed in churches, it is likely included in the context of confirmation or discipleship training. Yet, for example, a study by the Evangelical Lutheran Church in America's research and evaluation unit found that only one-third of the ELCA's congregations addressed the topic of stewardship within their confirmation program.[30]

Why have most congregations in many faith traditions failed to address issues of giving with young people? What gets in the way? The next chapter examines those questions.

# CHAPTER 3

# Obstacles to Addressing Money and Giving with Youth

Why aren't congregations talking about money and giving with young people? What gets in the way of a focus on youth giving?

We asked congregational and national leaders to reflect on those questions. We also looked at some of the broader literature on money and giving. In that process, we identified seven obstacles to a congregational focus on money and giving with youth. While these barriers may be higher in mainline Protestant and Catholic congregations (and some may be unique to those situations), congregations from all traditions would do well to reflect on whether these barriers are relevant to their situation.

It becomes clear in reviewing the obstacles to youth giving that most are also obstacles to giving among adults. This reality points to the broader challenge of recognizing that youth work needs to be seen not as an isolated set of programs but as integrally connected to the congregation's systems, activities, climate, relationships, and identity.

## OBSTACLE 1:
### DISCOMFORT WITH TALKING ABOUT MONEY

"When I was a kid, I was instructed not to talk about politics, religion, money, or sex," said Dwight Burlingame of Indiana University's Center on Philanthropy. "Today we talk about sex, we talk about religion in many different kinds of ways, and we talk about politics . . . but we still don't talk about money."

The silence about money is by no means universal. There is evidence that ethnic congregations (particularly with new immigrants) and congregations in low-income communities are more open about money issues.

In the case of new immigrant congregations, this attitude is, in part, a transfer from parts of the world where openness about money is normative. In other cases, such as African-American churches, it appears to grow out of a strong sense of communal accountability.[1]

However, most people simply don't want to talk about money at all, much less with young people. Robert Wuthnow's survey of American adult workers found that the vast majority had rarely discussed their personal finances with people outside their immediate family. The area that they were least likely to have talked about was their giving to charities. Ninety-two percent said they had never or hardly ever talked about this issue outside the family. Furthermore, the people they were least likely to talk with about personal finances were fellow church or synagogue members.[2]

One could anticipate considerable resistance from many quarters to bringing up the topic. Consider the following:

- A Yankelovich survey of American adults for Lutheran Brotherhood found that 49 percent of Christians believe that it is inappropriate to discuss money and material possessions at their place of worship.[3]
- A survey by Wuthnow of 2,000 working adults in the United States found that 30 percent of the churchgoers said they would be less likely to give if their congregation were to place more emphasis on giving.[4]
- A study by empty tomb, inc., found that 85 percent of Christian clergy disagreed or strongly disagreed that "most pastors enjoy preaching about money."[5]

While these surveys focus on Christians, some observers see similar patterns in the Jewish community. "Many of us have become comfortable talking in community about issues of sexuality and inclusivity and bodily disabilities," suggested Rabbi Shawn Zevit of the Jewish Reconstructionist Federation. "Our need now is to become as comfortable talking about money. That's the Talmud's approach, to treat money and resources as openly as it does bodily functions and relationships. But it's not so easy in our communities, where there are sometimes strong anti-institutional feelings associated with the money culture of organized Jewish life."[6]

What's the source of this discomfort and resistance to dealing with money in religious institutions? We asked youth workers, youth, and adults from several congregations in Indiana and Minnesota why they think money is a taboo subject in congregations. Some of the things they said:

- Money is a private thing.
- People are embarrassed about what they have, what they give, and what they could give.
- People feel that they're bragging.
- Many youth workers haven't developed good financial habits or habits of giving, so they're uncomfortable bringing up the subject with the youth.
- Money is a status symbol. It's a way to gauge success in our society.

Rabbi Arthur Waskow, a leader in the Jewish renewal movement writes:

In American Jewish life (and perhaps among Americans generally) there seems to be a very strong taboo against the frank and open discussion of how much money people have, how much they make, how much they want to give to charity, and so on. If those with more and with less money try to talk together, strong suspicions and resentments come to the surface. The rich feel concerned that those with less money will resent them and/or hit them up; the poor feel embarrassed and humiliated, or angry and rebellious.[7]

Many of the norms may grow out of what Wuthnow describes as "the privatization of money" in which people have a sense of being "radically alone." He writes: "We assume great responsibility for our money, but we receive little support from other people of the kind that might help us make better decisions or feel more confident about the decisions we do make. . . . Without the capacity to compare our thoughts and feelings with those of our peers, both our fantasies and our fears run wild."[8]

We do not have data on how much young people talk about money, financial choices, and giving within their congregations, but there is little reason to believe it is significantly different from adult customs. While youth workers complain about the unquestioned materialism they see in many young people, our contacts with congregations suggest that young people rarely have opportunities to examine their use of money within the context of their faith community.

Evangelical author and professor Tony Campolo shares that perspective: "Seldom do we challenge kids to do anything Christian with their money," he said in an interview with *Youthworker Journal*. "But we fret about how to break money's hold on young people. I'm not convinced it has much of a hold on them. I have a feeling they're that way because churches—and specifically youth workers—have not presented them a viable alternative, an attractive lifestyle that makes sense in the kind of world we live in. If we don't challenge these kids to think seriously about money, we can't talk to them about other forms of discipleship."[9]

## OBSTACLE 2:
### LOSS OF LANGUAGE AND TRADITION TO MOTIVATE GIVING

Despite a rich heritage, many of the practices that taught giving have either been neglected or lost their meaning for many adherents, particularly among mainline Protestants and Catholics. Wuthnow writes: "There is a kind of mental or emotional gloss to contemporary religious teachings about money that prevents them from having much impact on how people actually lead their lives."[10]

A notable case in point is the word "stewardship," the most widely used term for giving and fund-raising in Christian traditions.[11] Robert Wood Lynn, formerly of Lilly Endowment, notes that the language of "stewardship" was introduced into mainline Christian thinking in the late 19th or early 20th century to take the place of an emphasis on systematic benevolence or charity. This shift grew out of a pressing need to persuade members to become steady, regular supporters of mission efforts. The word "stewardship" sounded respectable and avoided the awkwardness of talking about money. And, at the time, it worked.

The problem, Lynn says, is that the concept has lost its edge. Many Protestants now "talk endlessly about gratitude, but very seldom talk about systematic giving the way in which the previous generations did. . . . We went from [the] obligation to tithe . . . to gratitude, but without a corresponding understanding of how gratitude involves obedience or a disciplined form of response."

Lynn's contention is supported by Wuthnow's survey of American adults. Wuthnow found that most adults had, at best, a vague understanding of the concept of stewardship. Even among the most active churchgoers, only 42 percent said the term was very meaningful to them.[12]

Loren Mead, founder of the Alban Institute, goes further, describing stewardship as "a most sacred cow." Whereas some people say it has deep theological meaning, "In reality the word is perceived to be a euphemism for fund-raising. This kind of doublespeak is genuinely confusing to laypeople."[13]

In addition to the loss of compelling language to motivate giving, there is also concern that the practices and rituals that support it have lost power as well. Alban Institute President James P. Wind worries that "the formative practices of faith" that historically have helped young people learn the importance of giving have been lost. "Most of those practices have either receded from life entirely or at least become increasingly less powerful in a culture where there are so many immediate appeals to just buy the latest thing or have the latest experience."

In contrast, some of the strength of giving in Jewish temples and synagogues, conservative Christian churches, and ethnic congregations is that they have maintained language and rituals that remain meaningful. For example, Anita H. Plotinsky shows how the expectation to give is woven into all aspects of Jewish life and rituals, from pledges on High Holy Days and other holidays and festivals to *tzedakah* boxes on family tables to gifts to the poor in honor of events throughout the life cycle, from birth to bar or bat mitzvah to marriage to honoring the dead.[14]

## OBSTACLE 3:
### COMPETING AND CONFUSING MESSAGES

The loss of language and traditions of giving has led to widespread confusion and disagreement about giving in general and youth giving in particular. Listening to young people and youth workers in congregations talk about money and giving uncovers conflicting opinions. Consider these questions, which are left unanswered in many congregations:

- *Why should young people give?* Should they give because they receive benefits (such as participation in programs)? Should they give out of thankfulness to God? Should they give because of a religious commitment or obligation? Why ask them to give money at all when they are already contributing their time through service?
- *Which young people should give?* Should only those young people

with jobs give? And why should young people give money when it's really their parents' money? Isn't that "double dipping"?

- *To what or whom should young people give?* Should they give primarily (or exclusively) to their congregation? Or should they focus on causes in the community and world? And what if they disagree with the congregation's programs and activities?

The first set of questions is theological. These questions grow, in part, from the blending of many traditions and motivations without bringing clarity or focus. James Hudnut-Beumler notes that some of these distinctions reflect different emphases in Christian churches that date back at least to the Protestant Reformation.[15] Yet because young people and congregational leaders rarely reflect and hold dialogues about these kinds of questions, young people are left with a mishmash of reasons for giving, none of which is compelling.

The second set of questions addresses the purpose of encouraging youth giving. If, on the one hand, giving is viewed primarily as a fund-raising method, a focus on those with the most disposable income might be appropriate. If, however, the focus is on cultivating the habitual practice of giving in all young people as a spiritual discipline or religious obligation, then encouraging all to give becomes a guiding principle. Furthermore, most Judeo-Christian traditions share a theological emphasis on recognizing the opportunity to give as a privilege, honor, or response of gratitude. Those perspectives seem to be latent if not dormant in most congregations.

The final set of questions is particularly salient for youth workers. In past generations the religious community organized its giving through centralized systems, either within a denomination or across denominations (such as the United Jewish Appeal or Church World Service). Individuals gave their gifts to their congregation, and congregations in turn paid a proportionate share to unified benevolence and outreach endeavors.

Such patterns are no longer the norm. Congregations are giving less to national and regional structures. Instead, each congregation selects what it will support, increasingly focusing on designated gifts and support for tangible, closer-to-home causes. Members increasingly think of money sent to the denomination as "payment for services," not as an efficient method for having an impact in the world.

Many people's reluctance to address financial giving with youth seems to grow out of ambivalence about the appropriateness of giving to support religious institutions. (This issue is less relevant in the Jewish community, where dues to support the temple or synagogue are clearly separated from other fund-raising appeals for the Jewish community or other needs in the world.) Tony Campolo's blunt statement represents a widespread sentiment: "One of the worst things to tell kids is that they should give money 'to the church.' Most kids are uptight about the way churches spend money. They're not particularly thrilled with the new carpet, the new tile on the roof, the new addition to the sanctuary."[16]

While congregational leaders and youth workers know that it costs money to run a congregation, they aren't sure how that fits with the religious imperative to give to others. (By one estimate, approximately 70 percent of contributions to congregations are used to pay staff salaries, expenses related to activities within the congregation, and other operational costs,)[17] As Roman Catholic Bishop William E. McManus has said: "The concept of alms has been lost. People think when they give to the church, it's alms. I tell them, 'You're kidding—you get it all back: air conditioning, four priests, eight staff, a musician.' Almsgiving traditionally is where the person gives and receives nothing in return from the one benefited."[18]

Others dislike the dichotomy between spending on the congregation and spending on benevolence, suggesting that it places an unnecessary value judgment on the congregation's programs and activities. "As I understand church life," writes Loren Mead, *"everything a church does is supposed to be outreach.* The worship is outreach. The parish education program is outreach. Every activity of the congregation should be dedicated to strengthening its members for outreach and supporting activities of outreach. . . . One hundred percent of a congregation's energy and resources should be engaged in outreach, not 10 or 20 or even 50 percent."[19]

The difficulty of addressing the mixed messages about money and institutional realities only makes it more important that congregations address these and other money-related questions directly and honestly with youth and adults. Doing otherwise only adds to the confusion, false assumptions, and mixed messages that interfere with thoughtful, disciplined, and reflective giving by people of all ages. Better approaches are to:

- Acknowledge and talk with young people about the discomfort, ambivalence, and awkwardness of addressing institutional needs
- Begin congregationwide introspection about the congregation's mission, how it is supported financially, and how to balance institutional needs with community and global needs

- Engage young people in reflection, conversation, and education about their responsibilities to support their religious institutions and how they can be trustees and stewards of these institutions
- Find ways to balance pressing financial needs with a long-term perspective of youth as future givers

## OBSTACLE 4:
## AN EXCLUSIVE FOCUS ON INSTITUTIONAL NEEDS

Mainline Christian congregations and denominations face critical challenges, prompting Loren Mead to worry about a "financial meltdown in the mainline." Analyzing a wide range of data and trends, and listening to leaders in many denominations, Mead worries (among other things) that "hundreds of congregations [will face] the loss of 20 to 50 percent of their pledged income in the next fifteen to twenty years."[20]

The situation is uncertain in other traditions as well, even those that historically enjoyed higher levels of giving. Jewish leaders worry that more and more American Jews are loosening their bonds to Jewish institutions, including synagogues and temples, raising questions about whether these institutions will have, in the long term, the support to sustain their efforts. Barry A. Kosmin of the Council of Jewish Federations in New York noted in 1995 that the United Jewish Appeal/Federation annual campaign, though impressive in its total, actually lost ground (in real, inflation-adjusted dollars) in each of the two previous decades.[21]

Operational issues are a major source of frustration for youth workers as well as the larger institution, contended Mark Vincent of the Giving Project. He said that youth workers "are also getting quite stressed over the amount of funds and fund-raising activities that it's beginning to require. . . . Typically what I hear is someone saying, 'I didn't go to college or train for youth ministry in order to be a professional fund-raiser. And it seems like that's all I'm doing.' . . . It just becomes one additional area in the church where the money side of it is purely operational and not thought about theologically."

The urgency of addressing financial issues that threaten the survival of many religious institutions at a local, regional, and national level cannot be overstated.[22] A number of recent publications provide grist and direction for examining these needs.[23] Yet it is important not to become so focused on crisis management that the underlying issues and long-term solutions are ignored or neglected. In three areas an exclusive focus on institutional needs can become an obstacle to youth giving:

### FOCUS ON CURRENT NEEDS, NOT LONG-TERM HEALTH

A focus on current institutional needs does not cultivate givers for the long term, namely youth and young adults.

Congregations seem to hold to the maxim to "go where the money is" and focus their fund-raising efforts on members who are wealthy or otherwise fit the profile of people who give the most. This focus likely has short-term benefits in paying the bills or meeting new challenges. Lutheran Brotherhood's Nathan Dungan said: "They are so focused on today, the immediate, that they haven't thought about the child as a future giver." And because young people don't contribute at levels that would address current financial crises, "they don't get a lot of attention."

### FOCUS ON RAISING FUNDS, NOT DEVELOPING FAITH PRACTICES

An exclusive focus on institutional needs can undermine a clear, challenging focus on individual giving as a spiritual discipline or religious obligation. Mark Vincent argues that the emphasis on institutional needs is a major barrier to a healthy understanding of giving:

> We are still in a place where congregations set a budget and say that's our stewardship benchmark. If we reach this arbitrarily decided dollar amount, we have been good stewards. . . . So what a child grows up with in a congregation . . . is, "Here's the amount we need; help us meet it," rather than, "Generous God, generous life." So on the whole, if you look for the drumbeat of stewardship, this tape recording that is always playing in the background . . . does not even agree with Christian theology. It is operational, rather than theological, and they are not congruent.

Many observers suggest that the financial problems are integrally related to fundamental questions of religious identity and spirituality. Loren Mead writes: "The financial crisis we are approaching is part of a larger spiritual problem we have in America's churches: our inability to deal honestly with our own wealth. This is a spiritual and theological problem . . . I think we are doing a poor job on the first issue [institutional finances], because we have not been willing to face the second."[24]

## BUREAUCRATIZATION OF GIVING

In her examination of philanthropy in the Roman Catholic Church, Mary J. Oates argues that an important factor in the decline in Catholic giving has been the increased bureaucratization and centralization of the church's benevolence efforts. "As bureaucracy, clerical dominance, and reliance on government funding developed after 1920," she writes, "lay voluntary initiative waned."[25] By the 1970s, this pattern was being reinforced by the use of centralized, professionally run annual fundraising campaigns to meet all diocesan needs.

While Oates's focus is on the Catholic Church, the pattern is widespread across faith traditions. While these approaches may increase the revenues generated, but also make giving more abstract and distant for young people. According to the youth workers and congregational leaders we interviewed, those qualities make it very difficult to encourage giving among youth, who tend to be motivated to give to address specific, concrete needs, not out of a compelling loyalty and commitment to the institution.

## OBSTACLE 5:
## LACK OF EMPHASIS, GUIDANCE, OR TEACHING

As suggested above, the almost exclusive focus on institutional needs has overshadowed the important questions about money, materialism, and giving from a faith perspective. "Because of the financial pressures it is under, the church is becoming increasingly effective in communicating the message about its fund-raising needs," said James Wind. "And yet, the church seems also quite silent about the personal and spiritual side of [money]." Focusing on institutional budget needs without also helping people develop a faith perspective on their economic lives, Wind said, "adds just one more pressure to people who are already feeling quite strapped and strained by the economic pressures of their lives."

This general pattern in congregations is replicated in youth programming. "Too many times I get stuff in the mail about fund-raisers," said Ohio youth worker Efrem Smith. "You know, like, 'If you want to do mission trips, hey, sell candy, sell this, sell that.' But, I don't get many resources across my desk that talk about helping kids take what they have and spend it wisely and not just spend 100 percent of their money on themselves but use some . . . to help others. . . . What about some ideas on how to talk to teens about how to take what they have and not just use it for themselves, but use it to impact others?"

Part of the challenge is that money and giving are not seen as core themes in Christian teaching, despite their prominence in Scripture. Daniel Conway of the Archdiocese of Indianapolis notes that the latest Catechism of the Roman Catholic Church, released in English in 1994, barely mentions stewardship and money.[26] Furthermore, only a few Christian denominations have developed curricula and resources for youth that address giving.[27]

The lack of teaching also leaves parents without the experience, practices, and knowledge that equip them to pass along faith-based values regarding money, including the practice of giving. Asked about barriers to youth giving, the Rev. Eileen Campbell-Reed of Heritage Baptist Church, Cartersville, Georgia, said: "I think the biggest barrier is that they're not being taught or having modeled for them what it means to give in their homes. . . . We have a lot of . . . parents who don't understand this concept [of giving], and they're not teaching it to their children."

Perhaps most troublesome in the long term, however, is that the lack of attention to financial issues with youth leaves them with no counterbalance to the materialistic, consumer-oriented culture that they face daily. Says Robert Wuthnow: "[People] are left with no outside advice other than what they receive from the mass media: buy this, buy that, spend more, focus on brands and prices, not whether to buy something at all."[28] Such a lack of guidance not only affects young people's giving; it also leaves them with little help making a wide range of financial decisions—from employment and vocation to saving and investing—based on their faith values, priorities, and beliefs.

## OBSTACLE 6:

## FINANCIAL ANXIETIES OF CLERGY AND YOUTH LEADERS

Robert Wood Lynn recalls a stewardship retreat he led several years ago with Presbyterian clergy. From the moment he arrived, he could tell that "the young ministers just hated the ideas, and I was really struggling up- stream." But then as participants listened to other clergy talk about their own indebtedness and financial struggles, Lynn realized that "they hated to talk about money because it reminded them of their own situation." In a focus group with youth workers, this issue was also a clear source of stress. Some of the leaders' discomfort grows out of unfamiliarity with today's complex financial world. Nathan Dungan put it this way: "I have observed that many clergy do not have a well-developed financial vocabulary, and, absent that, may feel inadequate in engaging people in critical financial con- versations. . . . One significant contributing factor is the lack of financial training clergy receive in seminary."

Clergy also struggle to link financial matters with faith. "Pastors . . . do not know how to discuss the theological implications and the spiritual impli- cations," contended Sylvia Ronsvalle. "They do not see stewardship as a spiritual discipline." Because congregations haven't dealt head-on with money, the church "doesn't carry a lot of weight . . . in this money-preoccu- pied society," she said.

The challenge, then, is that many of the areas where young people need guidance and support are areas where religious leaders have work to do themselves. Mead writes: "Clergy do not need 'head' knowledge but 'heart' learning. They need to understand the emotional impact of money in their own lives and the lives of others. They need to know why they feel uncomfortable talking about money when Jesus talked about it more than any other topic he is recorded as having talked about."[29]

## OBSTACLE 7:

## BELIEF THAT YOUTH SHOULDN'T BE EXPECTED TO GIVE

The people we interviewed identified a number of different why young people shouldn't be asked or expected to give money. Some reasons are grounded in difficult dilemmas for congregations. Others reflect widespread misperceptions in congregations and the culture of young people and their place in the world.

## Youth Don't Have Any Money

In chapter 2, we highlighted the amount of money that marketers now say young people have. But youth and religious leaders maintain that a lack of money is still a big reason why young people don't—and shouldn't—give. "One of the things that [youth] see as a barrier is that they think they don't have any money," said Eileen Campbell-Reed. "And the truth is . . . they have more disposable income right now than teenagers ever had [before], . . . and yet they don't see that any of that could be set aside or used for the church."

The notion that young people don't have anything to give stands in sharp contrast to their spending habits. "We have instances all the time where kids will spend a fortune on a particular pair of jeans or shoes or rock-concert tickets or a CD or whatever, and think nothing of it," said Jules Gutin of the United Synagogue of Conservative Judaism. "But when there's a USY [United Synagogue Youth] weekend . . . that's for, like, $40 including the food, they'll complain that it's too expensive."

When posed with the idea that youth shouldn't be asked to give because those that don't have money will feel bad, John and Sylvia Ronsvalle responded this way:

SYLVIA: Oh, interesting. When we go into churches and we say that you ought to take giving seriously, they say, "Oh, there are so many people on fixed incomes, and we shouldn't talk about it because the old people will feel bad.

JOHN: And the newlyweds are just buying their homes. And the middle-aged people . . .

SYLVIA: And so the upshot is: It is never convenient to talk about money. And the point is that the embarrassing thing about religion is that God doesn't seem to hold off, even in light of these very valid reasons.

Many observers also note that whether or not young people have money is not really the point. Most faith traditions don't limit responsibility for meeting the needs of others only to the rich. Everyone is asked—or mandated—to give to others according to her or his means. Consider these two statements:

- "Even a poor person who is kept alive by *tzedakah* funds must give *tzedakah* from what he receives." (Shulchan Aruch, Yoreh De'ah 251:12)
- "[Jesus] looked up and saw rich people putting their gifts into the treasury; he also saw a poor widow put in two small copper coins. He said, 'Truly I tell you, this poor widow has put in more than all of them; for all of them have contributed out of their abundance, but she out of her poverty has put in all she had to live on.'" (Luke 21:1-4)

## BEING ASKED TO GIVE MAY ENCOURAGE THEM TO LEAVE

Many Jewish and Christian congregations struggle simply to keep young people involved. Often they see a dramatic decline in attendance around ninth grade after key rites of passage such as bar or bat mitzvah or confirmation.[30] In this context, it seems counterproductive to many youth workers, parents, and other congregational leader to increase expectations of young people. As Dean Hoge put it, "Many middle-class people don't want to put any burdens on kids, so you don't want to introduce any 'oughts.'"

The challenge is similar, though somewhat different, for "seeker" congregations that focus on attracting young people who haven't been active. Thom Schultz of Group Publishing said he wonders if, in the minds of some youth workers, a commitment to outreach may conflict with a focus on giving. "Talking a lot about financial giving when kids come in the door . . . may turn off those whom you are trying to evangelize. If they hear the first time they visit an appeal for them to dig into their pockets, well, . . . they might not come back next Sunday because of that pressure . . . to give financially."

What this perspective misses is that young people want to be challenged, want to make a difference, want to contribute. To be sure, asking newcomers to give may be inappropriate, particularly if giving is seen as "payment for services" and not as a response or obligation of faith. But if congregations truly believe that financial giving is part of a growing, maturing faith commitment, then it should not be neglected as part of efforts to help young people grow.

## YOUTH NEED TO SAVE

A participant in a youth focus group was clear: "You need to save for college and stuff. College is expensive, and we need money for that. But after you get out of college, you should start giving then." Another young person said: "All my money goes into my savings account. That is my budget."

Mark Vincent of the Giving Project consistently sees saving emphasized to the exclusion of giving. "When I talk with [young people], I'll just say, 'What do people ask you to do with your money?' And I'll start the sentence 'Save it . . . ,' and they all shout back at me 'for college.' So the whole energy for them around money that comes from family, friends, and the faith community is to get that education and save money for it—and to get a job that pays good money. And so this already is going in the wrong direction as far as I'm concerned for developing the kind of economic habits that are 'generous God, generous life.'"

## PARENTS OF YOUTH ALREADY GIVE

People worry that asking youth to give really just means that "parents pay twice." Part of the challenge comes in the mechanics of how congregations seek and account for gifts. "It's kind of awkward in churches because so many churches operate around a pledge system, and families make their pledges, " Wuthnow explained. "So it's not quite clear what the role of youthful giving should be."

The danger, of course, in this assumption is that it undermines one of the most powerful influences on young people's giving behaviors: the parents' own giving and expectations for giving. Indeed, parents who are consistent givers are most likely to be allies in efforts to encourage young people to give. The parents who resist are more likely to be those who have not themselves developed the habit of giving.

## YOUTH SHOULDN'T GIVE BECAUSE THEY'RE TOO YOUNG

Arva Rice of Public Allies in New York City said she hears people say: "We shouldn't be burdening them with [giving]. Give them an opportunity for kids to be kids. They shouldn't have to worry about paying for the furnace of the church." She suggested that this perspective reflects a paternalistic, condescending bias toward youth. "So they are always going to be the recipients."

Others highlight the inconsistency between beliefs and practices. "Do we really see young people as full members of our congregations?" asked LeRoy Wilke of the Lutheran Church–Missouri Synod. "I think a lot of people would say yes to that, but have a hard time when you push the question: . . . 'Well, what about stewardship? Are we intentional about talking with young people, or do we just talk with their parents about stewardship?'"

In contrast to much conventional wisdom, there may be practical, economic reasons for getting teenagers into the habit of giving while they are still young. Robert Wuthnow said he worries that not teaching young people about giving now "can be kind of a cumulative effect, too, as one generation doesn't pass along those values to another." He suggested that establishing a habit of giving early in life sets the stage for a lifetime of giving. "So it's a much richer payoff in sheer economic terms than if you teach an 80-year-old to give." But that's not the only reason. "The lowest rates of giving are among young adults," he noted. "So if you want to do something about that, one thing is to work on the young adults themselves. But the other is to work on them before they get to be young adults and try to establish the pattern."

There are, of course, differences in how one would address giving and other financial issues with younger and older adolescents, for both developmental and practical reasons. Younger ones, on average, have less money and relatively fewer financial choices than older teenagers. Thus, young adolescents can learn the basic habits and principles without some of the pressures they will face as they grow older. With their increased mobility, expenses (cars, dating), credit cards, and increased time demands (particularly if they work), older youth are ready for deep reflection regarding vocation, priorities, and life commitments.

## OPPORTUNITIES FOR POSITIVE CHANGE

We've looked at seven obstacles, some of them huge. They raise fundamental questions not just about youth work but also about the health and future of religious institutions. They highlight a need to focus not just on giving, but also on deep-seated, difficult questions about money, materialism, values, and culture. They challenge congregations to think differently about the role of young people. While the obstacles may be daunting, there are also important opportunities for moving forward. Let's look briefly at these.

## EARLY SIGNS OF INTEREST

Early signs suggest an increasing interest in addressing youth giving in congregations and denominations. Some of this interest may have been kindled by the ironic intersection of a booming economy and financially struggling religious institutions. Some of it may be related to widespread concern about the seeming fragility of the philanthropic tradition, as wealth passes by inheritance from one generation to another. Some of it may reflect the visibility of the efforts to examine financial issues in religious institutions that were part of the Lilly Endowment's Financing American Religion initiative.[31] Whatever the causes, an incipient interest examining youth giving is evident. When we brought up the topic with youth workers, many said: "I don't know much about that and haven't done much. But please let me know what you find out."

## STRONG TRADITIONS AND CONGREGATIONS

Some readers may have had trouble identifying with the list of obstacles in this chapter. For most Jewish congregations, for example, a focus on youth giving is a natural, ongoing part of faith. These congregations (some of which are featured in this book) and the traditions upon which they stand have much to teach others, both about the traditions that guide them and the practices that sustain them.

## WILLINGNESS TO GIVE WHEN ASKED

When young people are encouraged and asked to give, they are often willing—even eager—to do so, according to those leaders who have engaged young people in giving. "Our experience in [United Synagogue Youth] is that kids *are* willing to make a financial contribution," said Jules Gutin of the

United Synagogue of Conservative Judaism. "This past year our kids raised over $300,000 for our charity program. This is similar to the amounts raised on an annual basis for at least the past five years."

## WE'VE BEEN HERE BEFORE

A prominent Christian leader once wrote of an era "of church entertainments and religious amusement. . . . It was supposed in so many churches that young people especially must be coaxed and wheedled into being religious." He described a range of self-improvement activities, entertainment, and other events that were "often relied upon to win young people to the church" and to keep them loyal to the congregation. Yet, despite early successes, the novelty of these approaches quickly wore off. "Those that were thus attracted proved of little value to the church; the deeper springs of their natures evidently were not touched, and their enthusiasm for the service of Christ was not aroused."

What time period does the quotation describe? It could be the last two decades of the 20th century, when congregations struggled to keep young people connected and engaged. Yet the description in fact dates to the 1880s, not the 1980s. The author was the Rev. Francis Edward Clark, founder of the Society of Christian Endeavor, a movement in the late 19th century to make "young people more useful in the service of God and more efficient in church-work, and thus establish them in the faith and practice of the gospel."[32]

In contrast to a widespread assumption that the church had to entertain young people to keep them involved, Clark challenged them with "strenuous" expectations to contribute. Instead of turning off young people, this movement attracted at least 10 million followers. Among other things, the society established "the Tenth Legion," which encouraged young people to give 10 percent of their money "for the advancement of God's cause either in their own country or in foreign lands."[33]

More than a century later, many congregations are, once again, struggling to find ways to attract and keep young people involved. A common strategy is to compete by "one-upping" other choices, making it more fun or easier to be involved in congregational youth activities. Yet, as with the Christian Endeavor movement of a century ago, the real hope and possibility may lie not in lowering expectations, but in raising them, believing that young people will rise to the challenge. For evidence, we need only to look to the field of youth service.

## THE RISE OF YOUTH INVOLVEMENT IN SERVICE

Finally, a key opportunity for reinvigorating a focus on youth giving is that congregations have rediscovered the power of engaging young people in service—not only to make a difference in the world, but to transform their lives. They have dispelled myths that young people don't have much to give, that they don't want to get involved, that they'll be turned off by high demands. In fact, the opposite is true, and youth service is becoming a key focus of youth work in congregations across many faith traditions. Congregations are seeing how engaging young people in service to others often becomes a catalyst for reinvigorating and transforming a congregation.

# CHAPTER 4

# Serving Others:
# An Emerging Emphasis

Whereas adults may express concern that teenagers don't have money to give, they celebrate the many ways young people contribute through service. Whereas members often think financial giving should be reserved for adults, they see young people taking the lead in service in their synagogues, churches, and temples—sometimes bringing the adults with them. Whereas church leaders often worry that asking young people to contribute money will scare youth away, they have seen how inviting teenagers to serve attracts them and keeps them connected.

Indeed, youth service (which we use as an inclusive term to include social action, activism, voluntarism, service-learning, and missions) has become an important part of religious youth work, public education, and the whole field of youth development. Young people have numerous opportunities to serve, and many are involved. However, barriers persist, and service opportunities within congregations sometimes fall short of their potential.

## THE GROWTH OF YOUTH SERVICE INVOLVEMENT

Many of the people we interviewed said that today's young people seem to be more attuned to issues of service and justice. A survey for Prudential Insurance Company of America found that 95 percent of youth believed it was very or somewhat important for youth to learn the value of community service.[1] Similarly, a Gallup Youth Survey found that nine out of ten teenagers say that doing charitable or volunteer work is an important or very important part of being a good citizen.[2]

Multiple factors may account for this interest. Thom Schultz argues that the high interest in service reflects "a counterbalancing effect with some of the other things that are happening in society today that are making service and helping others more attractive and more logical for kids to be interested in." He pointed to the effect of technology, which creates "a counterbalancing hunger for human relationships, . . . to reach out more in a personal and human way."

Another factor may be the increased emphasis on service in many parts of society. Widespread efforts to engage young people in service or volunteering developed in various settings in the last two decades of the 20th century. By the end of the 1990s, involvement in service had become something of an expectation for youth. Forty percent of high school respondents in the Prudential Spirit of Community Youth Survey said their school emphasizes volunteering. One-third of youth (32 percent) said their parents and other family members emphasized volunteering.[3]

Some of this focus developed in response to a widespread perception of youth complacency and disengagement in the 1970s. Schools, youth organizations, and congregations have increasingly made service an integral part of programming or curriculum. Furthermore, beginning in the early 1990s, national organizations and policy makers began generating significant public and policy support (and funding) for engaging young people in service, particularly school-based community service or service-learning (service involvement that includes an intentional focus on academic learning).[4]

The number of schools offering community service illustrates the growth and pervasiveness of service opportunities for young people. A 1999 report from the National Service-Learning Clearinghouse compared data on youth engagement in service in 1984 and 1997. In 1984, community service and service-learning were available in schools to slightly more than one-fourth of all high school students, with only 27 percent of high schools offering some sort of community service. Mainly white students were involved.

By 1997, the situation had changed significantly. By this time, 96 percent of schools offered some kind of service opportunities. What is most astonishing, however, is that the number of students involved in school-based service had climbed by 686 percent, from an estimated 900,000 students in 1984 to 6.1 million students in 1997. This wider involvement also reflected much more closely the diversity of the U.S. student population.[5] Search Institute identifies young people who spend an hour or more in an average week "helping other people without getting paid." Half of young people surveyed say they are engaged at service to others at this level[6] (see figure 4).

# Figure 4

## Levels of Youth Involvement in Service to Others

(Percentages of youth who report serving in the community one or more hours "during an average week," based on Search Institute surveys of almost 100,000 sixth- to 12-grade youth in 213 communities during the 1996-97 school year.)

| Total Sample | All Youth | 50% |
|---|---|---|
| Gender | Females | 55% |
|  | Males | 45% |
| Grade | 6th | 61% |
|  | 7th | 56% |
|  | 8th | 51% |
|  | 9th | 48% |
|  | 10th | 46% |
|  | 11th | 44% |
|  | 12th | 45% |
| Race/Ethnicity | American Indian | 49% |
|  | Asian American | 48% |
|  | African American | 49% |
|  | Hispanic American | 45% |
|  | White American | 50% |
|  | Multiracial | 51% |

SOURCE: Peter L. Benson, et al., *A Fragile Foundation: Developmental Assets Among American Youth* (Minneapolis: Search Institute, 1999), 18, 140.

This table suggests that involvement in service to others is fairly consistent across most racial/ethnic populations. However, there are some other important differences. Females are more likely than males to engage in service. And service involvement is lower for older students than for those in the middle grades.

Independent Sector surveys show important differences in levels of volunteering by religious affiliation. Only 40 percent of young people who had no religious affiliation volunteered in 1996. Sixty percent of Protestant Christian youth volunteered, compared to 63 percent of Catholic youth and 74 percent of youth affiliated with other religious traditions, including Judaism.[7]

The Monitoring the Future survey of high school seniors gives a slightly different picture. As shown in figure 5 on the following page, almost three-fourths of seniors say they are involved in some kind of community affairs or volunteer work. However, 42 percent say that they are involved only a few times per year.[8]

## CONGREGATION-SPONSORED SERVICE ACTIVITIES

Much of the growing emphasis on service in schools has been paralleled by a growing emphasis on service to others as an integral part of congregational youth work. It has also become a major part of the programming of denominations and national organizations engaged in religious youth work. Religious institutions provide a significant number of the volunteer activities for young people, and they are an important "entry point." Among young people who volunteer, 53 percent first learned about volunteer activities through their congregation. In comparison, 50 percent learned about activities through their school, 22 percent through a youth organization, 20 percent through a community group, and 47 percent through other settings.[9]

Many of the congregations we contacted are working to tap into this interest in serving others, making service a central part of their youth work. Ginghamsburg United Methodist Church, a megachurch in Tipp City, Ohio, may exemplify the many ways service becomes integral to youth work. According to Efrem Smith, the youth pastor, the congregation sponsors at least four mission trips each year, as well as a local effort through which young people do mentoring, tutoring, and running Bible clubs with children. He explained: "Teens ... can have an opportunity at least four times a year

**Figure 5**

## High School Seniors' Time Spent Serving Others

(Percentages of high school seniors who say they participate in community affairs or volunteer work, by level of involvement, according to the 1995 Monitoring the Future survey of 2,650 high school seniors.)

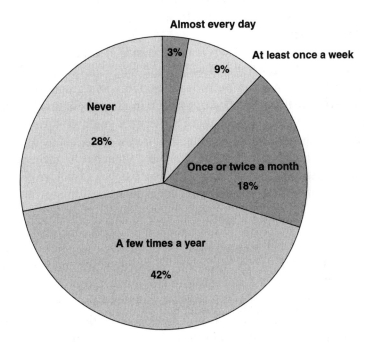

SOURCE: Lloyd D. Johnston, Jerald G. Bachman, and Patrick M. O'Malley, *Monitoring the Future: Questionnaire Responses from the Nation's High School Seniors, 1995* (Ann Arbor, Mich: Institute for Social Research, University of Michigan, 1997), 86.

to go on national [or] international mission trips. And then they have opportunities all year round to serve communities. . . . Teens have been involved in refurbishing homes [or] have gone down and volunteered in soup kitchens. So we see mission and serving as vital. It's like the heartbeat of the youth ministry here."

Service opportunities in and through congregations are widespread, but not universal. And, as in other settings where young people serve, not all young people who affiliate with a congregation are involved in its service activities. Yet many of the observers with whom we spoke said they've seen a noticeable increase in the focus on youth service in congregations in the past 20 years.

For example, one observer of the trends in youth service in Christian churches is Thom Schultz, president of Group Publishing, which has been sponsoring summer work camps for church youth groups since 1977 and included more than 12,000 young people in camps in summer 1999. "When we began, [service] was a natural activity for youth groups from mainline churches, because mainline churches have always had as a hallmark social justice kinds of things," he recalled. "What has happened over the 20 years is that mainline churches no longer have an exclusive clutch on it as they once did. Now everyone is just as interested in service, especially with kids."

## OPPORTUNITIES TO SERVE THROUGH CONGREGATIONS

Young people get involved in serving others or doing volunteer work through their congregation in many ways. These opportunities within congregations suggest how pervasive volunteering has become in religious youth work. They also raise important questions about how service is defined, what it includes, and how various types of service or volunteering have different kinds of impact.

### WITHIN THE CONGREGATION

Much congregation-based youth service centers on the congregation's programs and members. Indeed, 24 percent of all youth volunteer work counted in Independent Sector's research is service within the congregation.

This category includes teaching in religious education (6 percent), being a choir member (4 percent), and being an aide to a minister or rabbi (3 percent). Furthermore, 37 percent of young people surveyed said they had done volunteer work at a church or synagogue in the past year, compared to 35 percent who said they had worked on a community service project.[10]

In some senses, this area of service within the congregation raises the same kinds of questions that surfaced when discussing young people's financial contributions. How much should congregations distinguish between time spent in volunteer activities within the congregation and service involvement that addresses needs in the neighborhood, community, or world? How are the goals different for each kind of service? How should they be balanced?

Within the congregation are also many opportunities to offer care or service to others—often by service to elderly or homebound members or caring for younger children. The annual Parent's Day Out at Bethlehem Lutheran Church in Minneapolis is a good example. Each year, the congregation's youth group provides child care and activities for children from six months old to sixth grade so that parents will have time to do Christmas shopping. The teenagers help the children bake cookies and make cards for homebound members. Then the younger children deliver the cookies and cards while singing carols. Adults and older teenagers take the fourth- to sixth-graders shopping to buy toys for children who otherwise wouldn't get any (thus building a bridge to service in the community). The money comes from a fund-raiser coordinated by the fourth-graders.

## SERVICE IN THE COMMUNITY

Many youth get involved in service in their community through their congregation. Some volunteer on their own, asking for recommendations from leaders in their congregation. Others participate through service projects or activities operated or coordinated by the congregation. Examples of community service are plentiful: visiting nursing homes; providing after-school care to younger children; doing home repair, refurbishing, painting, and building; providing services for shut-ins; working in a food bank or soup kitchen, and tutoring. Many of these activities are tied to holidays, the ritual calendar, or the church year.

Most of these projects tend to be one-time or short-term commitments, particularly when they are done as group activities. However, some young people individually engage in long-term service commitments fostered through their involvement in the congregation. As one young person told us, "I have done a lot of community service through my synagogue, but most of the stuff I have done is just on my own."

## NATIONAL AND INTERNATIONAL WORK CAMPS

Work camps, work trips, mission trips, and trips to Israel tend to be the most visible and enticing service experiences for youth in many congregations. Not only do young people have opportunities to serve, but they like the chance to get away from home. Furthermore, the intensive, retreatlike closeness within the youth group over several days or a week can have a powerful bonding effect.

Opportunities for intensive work camp experiences abound. A Web search can locate literally hundreds of organizations sponsoring work camps for youth (as well as adults). Some organizations are religious; others focus on specific causes. Without exception, the leaders we spoke with in national organizations and denominations that offer work camp experiences have seen dramatic increases in participation across the past two decades. For example, Tom Bright of the Center for Ministry Development (which reaches primarily Catholic youth) says that the center's summer work camps, Young Neighbors in Action, have grown by 30 to 40 percent each year since they were begun in 1994. In 1999, the program involved almost 2,000 youth in 27 camps.

The merits of these kinds of experiences and whether they exploit residents of the communities helped is hotly debated. Some denominations, organizations, and activists have discouraged youth groups from participating in work camps on both ethical and practical grounds. On the ethical side, they note that the service projects can be designed more for the good of youth than for the community members being "served." They also note that important needs could be met closer to home, saving the significant costs of travel and allowing for ongoing relationships between the young people and the community served.

While proponents of work camp experiences agree that poorly planned experiences can be exploitative, they also believe that work camps can be planned thoughtfully and respectfully by agencies and community members working together to identify needs and projects. They say also that the novelty and adventure of planning and going on a trip is a major incentive for young people. That appeal simply is not available in local projects. In addition, a work camp can expose young people to other regions and cultures.

Finally, proponents of work camps highlight the benefits of giving young people and their leaders experience in effective service-learning through the intensive work camp—experience that many groups then apply in their own community. "If kids are allowed to be exposed the first time around to something a bit more exotic that involves traveling beyond their own community," said Thom Schultz, "that turns them on to return home and serve at home."

Schultz also sees the experience having a powerful influence on the whole youth program. "When kids go out for one week of a concentrated dose of serving others," Schultz said, "what we have seen often happen is that that forms an engine for the entire rest of their ministry and for the entire rest of the year." The experience serves as a focal point for helping the group clarify "what they are about, what they stand for, and what they care about."

Tom Bright suggested the need for a more integrated understanding of the variety of service experiences and recognizing "what service outside one's community or more extended service can do." He continued: "Sometimes the best way to view the service that needs to be done in my own community is to step outside and to serve someplace else—and then come back and recognize the parallels or the difference in needs."

These benefits and perspectives, do not, of course, directly address the concerns of the skeptics. As with almost any congregational effort to serve people in need, there is a risk of paternalism and misunderstanding if care is not taken to engage service recipients meaningfully in planning a project and in building mutually respectful relationships.

## OBSTACLES TO INCREASING YOUTH SERVICE ENGAGEMENT

While service involvement is fairly widespread and diverse in congregations, it is by no means universal. The relatively low percentages of youth who are involved in ongoing, consistent service to others suggest that most young people are "exposed" to service, not "engaged" in it. Lee M. Levison of Nobel and Greenough School in Dedham, Massachusetts, explains the difference in a chapter about school-based service-learning:

*Exposure* is what most students experience during their involvement in community service. The vast majority of programs aim to
expose students to people who are less fortunate than they are—
people with whom they would not ordinarily come into contact.
*Engagement* implies intensity. In such programs, students take
service seriously, they are intellectually engaged, the school's approach is multidimensional, and the school genuinely cares about
service. . . . Engagement programs require more commitment from
their students than just fulfilling the required number of hours.[11]

Despite the growth in commitment to and emphasis on service in congregations, leaders continue to encounter obstacles or challenges to engaging youth more actively or effectively in service to others. Ten barriers
surfaced in our interviews and research.

## CONCERNS ABOUT QUALITY

While it is clear that engaging young people in service is fairly widespread
in congregations, there is much less evidence that such involvement is consistently rewarding, enriching, or effective. Writing from a Catholic perspective, Thomas Bright and John Roberto (of the Center for Ministry Development) critique much of what they see in congregations:

No component or program in youth ministry is more maligned or
misused than service. Too often service projects serve in the un-
rewarding role of a parish requirement for the sacrament of Confirmation or a school requirement for graduation or course grade.
Service becomes another "must" in the lives of youth. Many service projects are so poorly planned that they do more harm than
good to youth and the people they are trying to help. . . . It is hard
to believe this is what Jesus had in mind when he spoke of serving
the needs of others.[12]

## TIME PRESSURES

As is true with all youth activities, a lack of available time is often seen as an obstacle to engaging youth in service. In one survey, high school students indicated that time was the most important reason why young people don't volunteer (figure 6 on the following page). "Students today are just so busy with things that are going on in their lives," said Alan Ramsey of the Fellowship Evangelical Free Church in Knoxville, Tennessee. "They have extracurricular activities, major school stuff, sports, and various other Christian clubs that they're a part of, and so time is a huge, huge issue. I think it is the biggest issue."

The levels of time pressure likely vary by community and youth subculture. For example, the Rev. Don Ng of First Chinese Baptist Church in San Francisco wondered if the traditions of Asian-American cultures may exacerbate the time pressures. "Many of our young people are looking for extracurricular activities for self-enhancement," he said. "They have this extra-credit mentality: . . . If I were to join this club or attend summer school or improve myself, I would have a better chance of getting into U.C. Berkeley, for example, or Stanford. So there is an academic success motivation . . . to accumulate enough of these extra academic enhancements to get ahead."

The challenge is not just young people's time, but time to fit service within the scope of programming in the congregation. "Churches have too many things on their plates," said Jewell Dassance of the Congress of National Black Churches. As a result, she said, many use whatever time they have to teach the faith and "don't engage children in other outside activities." Dassance also noted that the time pressures on adults also make it difficult to expand service experience for young people. "Many [service activities] require that children be in the church after church, after school, or Saturdays," she says. "And many churches just don't have adult volunteers to supervise those types of activities."

## LACK OF PARENTAL SUPPORT

In some cases, a lack of support from parents can become a challenge. One issue is the level of commitment. Rabbi Neal Gold said: "Sometimes the kids come to temple with much more enthusiasm than their parents do.

## Figure 6

## Barriers to Youth Service Involvement: Youth Perspectives

(Percentages of young people who did not volunteer in the past 12 months who had said each statement was a reason why they did not volunteer.)

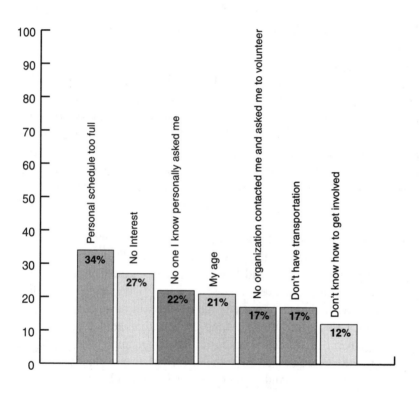

SOURCE: Virginia A. Hodgkinson and Murray S. Weitzman, *Volunteering and Giving among Teenagers 12 to 17 Years of Age: Findings from a National Survey. 1996 Edition* (Washington, D.C.: Independent Sector, 1997), 43.

. . . And sometimes kids who would want to be involved in anything and everything, don't get 100 percent reinforcement at home."

One reason parents may be less supportive, Gold suggested, is that the temple, like many other congregations, has not adequately addressed parent and family education. "We're just starting to talk about [more parent education], so I would want to figure out how to work *tikkun olam . . .* into the context of family education."

## ABSENCE OF ROLE MODELS

An important factor in shaping young people's commitment to and engagement in service is having role models to emulate. The role model can be a parent or another adult or a peer. Yet it appears that many young people don't have people they look to as role models in serving others. A 1995 survey of high school students found that only 50 percent could identify a particular person whom they admired for commitment to community service. Youth who volunteer are about twice as likely as nonvolunteers to be able to identify a role model (59 percent vs. 30 percent).[13]

## SELF-CENTERED CULTURAL NORMS

While service has become more common in schools and other settings, some youth workers still see that asking young to commit to serving others is countercultural. The Rev. Cherie Smith of Kirkwood (Missouri) Baptist Church puts it this way: "I think right now they're just so into being teenagers and doing what is cool and what is popular. And although their heart may tell them that this something they need to do, there's a lot of pressure out there to make other things a priority."

While individualism may, indeed, be an obstacle, Robert Wuthnow of Princeton University notes the paradox that emerged after the publication of the seminal work by Robert Bellah and his colleagues, *Habits of the Heart: Individualism and Commitment in American Life*.[14] "It kind of struck me," Wuthnow recalled, "that there was something a little bit peculiar or paradoxical about the fact that his group argued that we were so individualistic, and yet we seem to have the highest rate of volunteerism of any country in the world—at least that was the thought at the time."

That paradox drew Wuthnow into a deeper investigation of volunteerism. In *Acts of Compassion: Caring for Others and Helping Ourselves*, he asked: "How is it that we as a people are able to devote billions of hours to volunteer activities, to show care and compassion in so many ways to those around us, and still be a nation of individualists who pride ourselves on personal freedom, individual success, and the pursuit of self-interest? How do we reconcile these paradoxical elements in our tradition?"[15]

By the end of the book, he concluded that volunteerism is "not merely the manifestation of our most compassionate impulses but also an expression of our individualism. It allows us to carve up our caring in little chunks that require only a level of giving that does not conflict with our needs and interests as individuals," which may speak to why it is difficult to engage young people in more sustained service projects.[16]

## RACIAL AND CULTURAL BARRIERS

For the Chippewa-Cree youth of Our Savior's Lutheran Church, Box Elder, Montana, race is the biggest barrier, said the Rev. Joseph Bailey, senior pastor. "It's an issue for us, and it's an issue for the people we're trying to serve. . . . It's an issue for our kids because they are unsure about moving out among white society. They don't know quite how to do that real comfortably. It's an issue for the people we're serving—one, because oftentimes, they have never really dealt with Indian people. And, two, some of them are just plain outright racist. And we've encountered that."

Issues of race and culture can become serious barriers to service on several levels, particularly for youth from minority communities. Several factors come into play.

• The dominant white culture too often does not recognize or value these young people as a resource, viewing them more often as threats or problems based on stereotypes and misperceptions.

• The research on volunteering often undervalues or does not recognize some of the more informal expressions of care and service in many communities of color (such as helping a friend or a neighbor), which can lead to the misperception that youth of color are not interested in service.

• In the case of ethnic communities that also struggle with high rates of poverty, young people are often viewed paternalistically as recipients of services, not as contributors to the well-being of others.

Donald Ng described a culture clash that grows out of socioeconomic and generational differences within his congregation and between the congregation's youth group and its community. "We're a church that is made up of a lot of middle-class members," he said. "We're still located in a downtown neighborhood. In fact, we're right in the heart of Chinatown. . . . We have, on a daily basis, new immigrants coming to America and so it's a crowded place. But our young people, because they grow up in suburbs, . . . live outside of the center city. They want to serve, but there is a cultural clash. People who are economically or culturally or linguistically different from those who want to serve find this cultural chasm difficult to bridge."

## LACK OF INTEREST

As with so many other things, congregations often find that it's the same young people who are involved over and over. It can be very difficult to engage young people for the first time in service. "It's so frustrating," said Iowan Mary Kohlsdorff, "because you can't get kids to just do it once. . . . It's just getting kids to commit and take that first step. The ones that have taken that step, I have really seen their lives change."

## LACK OF EXPOSURE

Young people in middle- and upper-class communities where a veneer of self-sufficiency is a cultural norm can too easily lose sight of the need to serve others. Even though his temple is in an urban area of New Jersey, Rabbi Neal Gold described "living a sheltered suburban life" as an ongoing challenge. He noted that "we kind of mitigate [the isolation] a little by the fact that we're not a suburban *shul*—that we are in an urban setting. But, that doesn't mean that when you drive to temple that you necessarily see hungry homeless or desperate people on the way."

## LOGISTICAL CHALLENGES

Many youth workers and other leaders point to a variety of logistical issues that get in the way of actively engaging young people in service. These include:

- Individual or group transportation to the service destination either in or beyond the community.
- Funding to support the projects. Many groups spend a tremendous amount of energy on fund-raising, particularly to support projects beyond their community. Some youth drop out if they are expected to pay all or some of their expenses for these trips.
- Age restrictions on certain projects (such as home building or repair) by the sponsoring organization.
- Difficulty in recruiting adult sponsors to work with the young people.

## LACK OF INTEGRATION OF FAITH AND ACTION

While Jewish and Christian traditions clearly emphasize the religious roots of serving others, it's much less clear to what extent young people are motivated by the specific challenge of faith versus a general humanitarian sense of generosity or compassion. While basic generosity and compassion are worthwhile, they may not be adequate for transforming service into a faith-shaping, formative experience for young people.

Thom Schultz noted the missed opportunity when congregations "take their kids off and do a service project and perform some good work, and then simply go home." In his experience with Group Publishing's work camps (supported by research on effective service-learning),[17] an opportunity to reflect is essential for growth and learning, allowing young people to "reflect on what they have seen and what they have heard and what they have felt, and tie it back in to not only the rest of their lives, but also tie it back in . . . [to] our role as Christian people to serve others."

## MAYBE SERVICE AND GIVING AREN'T SO DIFFERENT

We began the chapter by noting the disparity between how giving and serving have taken root in congregational youth work. And, indeed, the commitment to youth service in congregations is much deeper than the commitment to financial giving, particularly in Christian churches. However, the differences may not be as polarized as we suggested. Consider, for example, the following:

- A major barrier to youth giving is a belief that young people don't have money to give. For service, the major barrier seems to be that they don't have time to give.
- One of the challenges for both giving and serving is a lack of role models among parents and other adults in the congregation or community.
- An important challenge in strengthening giving is to connect it to the traditions, beliefs, and sacred writings of the faith. A challenge for service is that young people may have only superficial motivations for serving (which will not sustain engagement) and may not have drawn deep connections to their faith and beliefs.
- The cultural emphasis on individualism and tending to one's own needs becomes a challenge for motivating both serving and giving.

# CHAPTER 5

# Rethinking Youth Giving and Serving

Chapters 2 to 4 summarized "the state of affairs" in youth giving and serving, highlighting both areas of strength and challenge. A logical follow-up question is "So what do we do about it?" A logical response to the question is to begin discussing how to design more effective programs for encouraging service and giving: How do you teach about giving and serving? What's the best curriculum to use? How can you offer more service projects? How can you start or strengthen a commitment to youth giving?

But wait! Each of these possibilities may have a place in encouraging young people to give and serve. However, focusing too quickly on the programmatic structure or solution misses the panoramic perspective on the factors that shape young people's generosity. And by addressing many of these factors, congregations can have a much greater impact in shaping teenagers' generosity.

Rather than focusing on what makes a service project or giving program effective, this chapter steps back to look at qualities and experiences during childhood and adolescence that make it more likely that young people (and adults) will be generous with their time and money. Then it examines a series of eight shifts needed in congregational life to move from the situation described in the three preceding chapters toward a community of faith that nurtures in its young people deep and lasting commitments to give and serve.

## The Roots of Generosity

To provide an important context for rethinking how congregations can encourage increased giving and serving among young people, let's examine what is known about factors identified by researchers that predict generosity in both youth and adults. This understanding can help shape strategies for improvement and change. Several explorations into the roots of generosity and caring give a sense of the range of factors that contribute to the development of generosity in children and youth.[1]

### Shaping a Moral Identity of Care

One of the leading scholars in philanthropy among adults is Paul G. Schervish, director of the Social Welfare Research Institute at Boston College. Through research on giving among the general population as well as in-depth research on wealthy Americans, he has identified six factors "especially important for inculcating a moral identity of care."[2]

- Participating in a group or organization (including school, congregation, or other setting) that expects or at least invites generosity. "Simply becoming involved in such organizations ends up creating a familiar setting in which we are spontaneously made aware of needs to which we may choose to respond," he writes.[3]
- Holding a "framework of consciousness"—such as religious beliefs—that shapes values and makes generosity a priority.
- Demonstrating and teaching generosity and charitable behavior to children, beginning at an early age, by parents or other admired adults.
- Receiving direct requests for involvement, many of which stem from participation in an organization. "Being asked by someone we know personally or by a representative of an organization we participate in is a major mobilizer."[4]
- Having discretionary resources of time and/or money. While Schervish notes that one's level of discretionary resources is "a mixture of objective and subjective considerations," he adds that "the amount of resources people are ready to give is in large part a function of how much they identify with and care for others in need."[5]

- Experiences or relationships during childhood or adolescence that inspire engagement. These contacts are "part of a moral education that molds our lives in a period when we are less guarded about our priorities and more apt to accrue at least a feel for the charitable impulse."[6]
- Experiencing intrinsic and extrinsic rewards that reinforce pro-social behavior and draw one deeper into a philanthropic commitment and identity.[7]

## LIGHTING A "COMMON FIRE"

Laurent A. Parks Daloz, Cheryl H. Keen, James P. Keen, and Sharon Daloz Parks published an important study in 1996, *Common Fire: Lives of Commitment in a Complex World*, which involved in-depth interviews with more than 100 adults who had dedicated their lives to the common good.[8] In analyzing the interviews, the researchers identified a number of common themes in the lives of these uncommon people:

- Growing up in a home that was loving, firm, respectful, and engaged with the world through activism, hospitality, service, and/or "vigorous discussions of current affairs"
- Having at least one sustained relationship with someone different from themselves
- Living in a neighborhood that provided both the safety in which to explore and discover, and the diversity to expose them to differences among people
- Being connected to a public institution (usually a school or congregation) that deliberately worked to create a sense of community and to link activities to the broader world
- Learning that "everyone counts" as they develop their own sense of confidence and ability to make a difference, and as they deepen their bonds to people different from themselves[9]

## Motivations for Giving and Volunteering

Beginning in the late 1980s, Independent Sector began a biennial series of national surveys of giving and serving among adults. Then, in 1990, the organization also began surveying young people on these same issues. A decade of these surveys has provided the most comprehensive statistical information base available on giving and behavior patterns.[10] Virginia A. Hodgkinson, Independent Sector's vice president for research (now retired), summarized factors identified in this research that increase the likelihood that youth and adults will volunteer and/or give:[11]

- Early, ongoing involvement in a religious group or other voluntary organization. "Whether teens or adults, those who were members of religious institutions or youth groups as children were far more likely to exhibit high levels of giving and volunteering later as teens and adults."[12]
- Role models at home and in the community. "Having witnessed members of one's family or another respected adult help others has a lifelong impact that grows more important with age. Young children particularly need to see adults they admire helping others."[13]
- Direct experience in serving others. "There is no substitute for the direct experience of volunteering. . . . Our surveys continue to show that volunteers are far more likely than nonvolunteers to be concerned about others and about social causes."[14]
- Being asked to give or serve. "Over eight out of ten teens and adults reported that they had volunteered when they were asked."[15]

In the Independent Sector report on teen volunteering and giving, researchers noted two important themes in predicting giving and serving among youth. The first is participation, which includes belonging to a youth group, doing volunteer work, doing door-to-door fund-raising, and being active in student government. The second is having role models—seeing someone in the family or someone else they admire help others. Nine out of ten youth who had volunteered in the past 12 months had both been active participants and had role models of generosity. Nine out of ten of the young people who made financial contributions in the past 12 months had also been active participants and had role models of generosity.[16]

## Building Developmental Assets

Beginning in 1990, Search Institute began an exploration of factors in young people's lives that contribute to healthy development. Surveys with more than a million 6th- to 12th-grade youth have consistently found that these factors, which we call developmental assets, are important building blocks for reducing problem behaviors (such as alcohol and other drug use, violence, and others) and also increasing the likelihood of positive behaviors, such as serving others, leadership, and appreciation of diversity.[17] Altogether, we have identified 40 developmental assets, which are listed and defined in figure 7 (on the following page).

The framework of developmental assets provides an important context for thinking about factors that contribute to a spirit of and a commitment to generosity. First, the framework recognizes that growing up generous is part of healthy development (see assets 8, 9, 26, and 27). In addition, it reminds us that a generous spirit is integrally linked with many dimensions of healthy development, not just with those experiences that are explicitly about caring or altruism. Indeed, the research consistently shows that the more of these 40 assets young people experience, the more likely they are to report regularly helping others.[18]

One way to understand the power of the assets to nurture generosity is to recognize within the asset framework many of the personal characteristics and socializing experiences that other researchers have found to be important in nurturing helping, caring, and generosity. For example, University of Massachusetts psychologist Ervin Staub reviewed three decades of his pioneering research on helping and altruism, identifying personal traits, parental socialization, childhood experiences, and sociocultural factors that shape caring. Figure 8 (page 87) links the factors he identifies with 18 of the 40 developmental assets.

# Figure 7

## Search Institute's Developmental Assets

Search Institute had identified the following 40 developmental assets (building blocks of healthy development) that help young people grow up healthy, caring, and responsible.

### External Assets

### Support

1. **Family support**—Family life provides high levels of love and support.
2. **Positive family communication**—Young person and her or his parent(s) communicate positively, and young person is willing to seek advice and counsel from parents.
3. **Other adult relationships**—Young person receives support from three or more nonparent adults.
4. **Caring neighborhood**—Young person experiences caring neighbors.
5. **Caring school climate**—School provides a caring, encouraging environment.
6. **Parent involvement in schooling**—Parents are actively involved in helping young person succeed in school.

### Empowerment

7. **Community values youth**—Young person perceives that adults in the community value youth.
8. **Youth as resources**—Young people are given useful roles in the community.
9. **Service to others**—Young person serves in the community one hour or more per week.
10. **Safety**—Young person feels safe at home, at school, and in the neighborhood.

### Boundaries and Expectations

11. **Family boundaries**—Family has clear rules and consequences and monitors the young person's whereabouts.
12. **School boundaries**—School provides clear rules and consequences.
13. **Neighborhood boundaries**—Neighbors take responsibility for monitoring young people's behavior.
14. **Adult role models**—Parent(s) and other adults model positive, responsible behavior.

15. **Positive peer influence**—Young person's best friends model responsible behavior.
16. **High expectations**—Both parent(s) and teachers encourage the young person to do well.

## Constructive Use of Time

17. **Creative activities**—Young person spends three or more hours per week in lessons or practice in music, theater, or other arts.
18. **Youth programs**—Young person spends three or more hours per week in sports, clubs, or organizations at school and/or in the community.
19. **Religious community**—Young person spends one or more hours per week in activities in a religious institution.
20. **Time at home**—Young person is out with friends "with nothing special to do" two or fewer nights per week.

## Internal Assets

## Commitment to Learning

21. **Achievement motivation**—Young person is motivated to do well in school.
22. **School engagement**—Young person is actively engaged in learning.
23. **Homework**—Young person reports doing at least one hour of homework every school day.
24. **Bonding to school**—Young person cares about her or his school.
25. **Reading for pleasure**—Young person reads for pleasure three or more hours per week.

## Positive Values

26. **Caring**—Young person places high value on helping other people.
27. **Equality and social justice**—Young person places high value on promoting equality and reducing hunger and poverty.
28. **Integrity**—Young person acts on convictions and stands up for her or his beliefs.
29. **Honesty**—Young person "tells the truth even when it is not easy."
30. **Responsibility**—Young person accepts and takes personal responsibility.
31. **Restraint**—Young person believes it is important not to be sexually active or to use alcohol or other drugs.

## Social Competencies

32. **Planning and decision making**—Young person knows how to plan ahead and make choices.

33. **Interpersonal competence**—Young person has empathy, sensitivity, and friendship skills.
34. **Cultural competence**—Young person has knowledge of and comfort with people of different cultural/racial/ethnic backgrounds.
35. **Resistance skills**—Young person can resist negative peer pressure and dangerous situations.
36. **Peaceful conflict resolution**—Young person seeks to resolve conflict nonviolently.

## Positive Indentity

37. **Personal power**—Young person feels he or she has control over "things that happen to me."
38. **Self-esteem**—Young person reports having a high self-esteem.
39. **Sense of purpose**—Young person reports that "my life has a purpose."
40. **Positive view of personal future**—young person is optimistic about her or his personal future.

## Figure 8
## Linking Caring to Search Institute's
## Framework of Developmental Assets

| Factors that Contribute to Caring* | Related to Developmental Assets** |
|---|---|
| **Parental Socialization and Childhood Experience** | **External Assets** |
| • Nurture and affection from family, teachers, and others. | • Family support (#1), positive communication (#2), other adult relationships (#3), caring neighborhood (#4), and caring school climate (#5). |
| • "Participation in creating rules and in decision making." | • Youth as resources (#8). |
| • Active participation in helping others. | • Service to others (#9). |
| • Guidance and essential rules for behavior in the family and in school. | • Family boundaries (#11), school boundaries (#12). |
| **Personal Characteristics** | **Internal Assets** |
| • Empathy, which involves "seeing and opening oneself to others' needs, understanding others' feelings, and feeling with others." | • Interpersonal competence (#33) and cultural competence (#34). |
| • "A commitment to moral rules and the resulting of obligation to help other people." | • Postitive values (#26-#31). |
| • A prosocial value orientation, which includes "a positive evaluation of human beings or human nature…a feeling for the concern for others' welfare…and a feeling of personal responsibility for the welfare of others." | • Caring (#26). |
| • A feeling of competence or power to help others. | • Personal power (#37). |

*Based on Ervin Staub, "How People Learn to Care," in Schervish et al., *Care and Community in Modern Society: Passing on the Tradition of Service to Future Generations* (San Fancisco: Jossey-Bass, 1995), 51-67.
**Based on Peter C. Scales and Nancy Leffert, *Developmental Assets: A Synthesis of the Scientific Research on Adolescent Development* (Minneapolis: Search Institute, 1999).

## Focusing on Religiosity and Congregations

Several of these frameworks have noted involvement in a faith community as a contributor to generosity and caring behaviors. However, these studies often simply emphasize the formative experiences that occurred within the congregation, not the unique accents and theological roots of the faith tradition. One review of studies on religion and caring by Search Institute President Peter L. Benson concluded that "religion . . . is related to caring, but in a manner we might call in the range of weak to modest."[19]

Too often, Benson suggested, social scientists simply stop looking at the role of religion. However, he noted that most studies are based on relatively superficial measures of religious involvement or a global statement regarding the importance of religion. Benson wrote:

> One can easily hold orthodox views, attend frequently, and claim importance, and yet hold a faith that is shallow, compartmental-ized, mechanical, and/or self-serving, in which religion's main function is to provide solace for the travails of life. At the other extreme, faith can be deep, dynamic, growing, integrated, and actively brought to bear on life's agendas and daily choices.[20]

With this in mind, Benson identified several dynamics regarding religious commitments and congregational life that more powerfully predict caring among young people.[21] These include:

- People of faith are more likely to engage in caring behavior if they have a religious worldview that challenges adherents to move into action, emphasizes a communal identity of "we" more than "me," and stresses the "horizontal" relationship between self and others. These perspectives are in contrast to religious world views that emphasize comforting adherents, individual identity, and a "vertical" relationship with the divine. (Most religious traditions have a mixture of the two.)
- In examining the dynamics of congregational life, several characteristics were most strongly associated with caring: an emphasis on teaching values, an emphasis on teaching a systemic perspective on world issues, a congregational climate that challenges young people to think for themselves, and concrete opportunities to practice caring for others[22]

## PUTTING IT TOGETHER

Several themes are fairly consistent across the preceding and other studies on giving and serving among youth and adults. Other accents are unique to a particular approach. To summarize some of the themes in the preceding studies, we suggest that being generous with time and money is shaped by many experiences, including:

- Experiencing the generosity of others and receiving care from parents and other significant adults
- Spending time in settings (home, congregation, school) where caring and generosity are invited and expected
- Being guided by religious beliefs (or other "frameworks of consciousness") that encourage (even mandate) care, compassion, and generosity
- Being in contact with mentors and role models (at home and elsewhere) who both practice and teach generosity
- Having concrete opportunities to serve and give—and being personally invited to participate
- Experiencing a faith that is alive, deep, dynamic—in short, life-shaping
- Finding enjoyment or fulfillment through acts of giving and serving
- Being connected to people from diverse backgrounds who have unique awareness of issues in the world
- Possessing self-confidence and a belief in one's own capacity to make a difference

This long list of factors speaks to an important theme that should be reinforced: There is no single event or strategy that, by itself, cultivates a lifestyle of generosity. Laurent A. Parks Daloz and his colleagues also capture this theme in *A Common Fire*:

> As we have discussed this study in a variety of public forums, people often ask for the single most crucial thing they can do to raise socially aware and responsible children. We do have a response for them, but it is important to say at the outset that there is no "Gandhi pill." No single event can ensure that a person will or will not live a life of commitment to the common good. It is a mix of key ingredients that matters. . . . In general, we have become

persuaded that the greater the number and depth of certain key experiences one has, the greater the probability of living a committed life.[23]

## EIGHT CULTURE SHIFTS FOR NURTURING GENEROUS YOUTH

All of the themes are relevant to how congregations shape their efforts to help young people grow up generous. Indeed, if they so choose, congregations can—and often do—influence or strengthen many of the factors identified in the research. And many congregations are effective in creating a culture that nurtures generosity.

However, as we saw in previous chapters, a great deal of room remains for re-examination and improvement. Indeed, the steady decline of contributions to congregations, the aging membership, and the perennial challenge of young people dropping out of congregational life during high school make change urgent: Urgent for congregations that could lose the vast resource that young people can offer both now and in the future. Urgent for youth who may otherwise be swept away by a culture that tells them to spend all their time and money on themselves. Urgent for a society and world that desperately need the contribution of young people's resources, creativity, energy, and commitment to bring about a more just and caring world.

What kinds of changes are needed for congregations to become more effective at helping young people grow up generous? It's not enough to think of new programs or simply "tweak" what's already going on. If the goal is truly to develop generations of young people who have instilled in them a lifetime commitment to giving and serving, the changes needed are systemic or cultural changes in congregations.[24] We have identified eight needed shifts, shown in figure 9. (This figure places each shift on a continuum that can be used for self-reflection about your own congregation.)

# Figure 9

## Eight Culture Shifts: A Tool for Reflection

This table sumarizes the eight culture shifts proposed in this chapter.
As you read the discusson of each shift, reflect with others in your
congregation on where your congregation is on the continuum between the
widespread realities suggested on the left side and the vision of a
congregation that is diligent about nuturing generosity in young people.

| | **From...** | | | **Toward...** | |
|---|---|---|---|---|---|
| 1. | Cultural Acquiescence | | | | Cultural Critique |
| | 1 | 2 | 3 | 4 | 5 |
| 2. | Immediate Opportunities | | | | Lifelong Generosity |
| | 1 | 2 | 3 | 4 | 5 |
| 3. | Youth as "Consumers of Services" | | | | Youth as Resources |
| | 1 | 2 | 3 | 4 | 5 |
| 4. | Programs and Curricula | | | | Relationships |
| | 1 | 2 | 3 | 4 | 5 |
| 5. | Fragmented Programs and Activities | | | | An Integrated Vision |
| | 1 | 2 | 3 | 4 | 5 |
| 6. | Isolation and Competition | | | Connections and Cooperation | |
| | 1 | 2 | 3 | 4 | 5 |
| 7. | A Few Young People | | | | All Youth |
| | 1 | 2 | 3 | 4 | 5 |
| 8. | Assumed Learning | | | | Intentional Growth |
| | 1 | 2 | 3 | 4 | 5 |

Depending on the congregation or faith tradition, some of these cultural changes are invitations to rediscover and recover historical and theological strengths. Others may be about adjusting to the new realities in the world. All are a matter of degree, not either/or choices. All suggest a direction for movement on a journey, recognizing that the change process may take years, decades, or even a generation.

## SHIFT 1:
### FROM CULTURAL ACQUIESCENCE TOWARD CULTURAL CRITIQUE

A life of generosity is countercultural life; it challenges many norms and expectations in a materialistic, market-oriented culture. Whereas the culture places self over others, a lifestyle of generosity calls for attention to the well-being of others and the common good. Whereas the culture sees the acquisition of wealth as an end in itself, a life of generosity sees wealth as a resource to be shared with others. Whereas the culture believes that "time is money" (and therefore must be carefully guarded), a life of generosity recognizes that time is the context for relationships and is itself a resource to be shared with others. Whereas the culture measures success in economic terms, a life of generosity finds meaning and value in human relationships and contributions to others and the world.

The faith community has, in too many cases, acquiesced to, been co-opted by, or embraced the culture of consumerism. Many leaders are quick to reinforce young people who place exclusive priority on saving for college (or a car) without sharing with others. Too often, congregations focus on meeting the self-interests of youth without inviting them to higher purposes and challenges. Too many leaders give up when young people place so much priority on a social life, working, or school activities that they "don't have time" to be generous—rather than engaging young people in dialogue about priorities and values. The point is not that those other things are bad. The problem is that their preeminence in young people's calendars and wallets is not examined.

Not all readers will agree with these statements. Life is more complicated than a series of yes-or-no judgments. However, the stark contrasts are intended to challenge congregations to reflect on their own practices, the subtle ways they reinforce or challenge norms in society, and how they can help to create a subculture in which young people both learn the practices of generosity and find support for living a generous life.

This is, of course, difficult work—particularly since topics like money and life tend to cause discomfort. Culture critique can create conflict. It can alienate members. It can be misunderstood and misinterpreted. But it can also offer the kinds of opportunity that people of all ages need to sort through the stresses and tensions they feel. It may be an opportunity for rediscovering the language and practices of the faith tradition that sustain people. It may be the opportunity to find support, kinship, and mutual accountability with others who are committed to living generously. In short, it may be the opening needed for discovering new, rewarding ways to live faithfully and generously in a complex world.

## SHIFT 2:
### FROM IMMEDIATE OPPORTUNITIES TOWARD LIFELONG GENEROSITY

For most youth workers and congregational leaders, the typical question is, How do we get more young people involved in the service project next week or the work camp next summer? While it is important to get young people involved in concrete opportunities to give and serve, a much more fundamental question is, What experiences and relationships do young people need now to form a foundation for a lifetime of generosity?

Ideally, those life-forming experiences should include repeated involvement in service and giving during childhood and adolescence. But nurturing generosity requires a broader perspective, highlighting the importance of connecting youth with caring, generous role models, experiencing a healthy family that is engaged with the world, and experiencing the congregation as a caring, challenging, nurturing community of faith.

While it may be important to begin having service projects or inviting young people to contribute financially, it may be just as (if not more) important to create a culture in the congregation in which young people feel valued and cared for, where generosity becomes a norm and expectation for all, and where the families are recognized as allies and partners in nurturing faith and generosity.

This long-term perspective is important also for another reason: Active, meaningful engagement won't happen overnight. Take the experiences of one congregation in Indiana, for example. As part of its efforts to encourage young people to give and serve, the church's youth planned a major service and awareness event, the 30-Hour Famine, a program developed by World Vision. The event—which had been highly successful the previous year—was to begin Friday evening with an all-night lock-in during which young people would fast and learn about hunger issues. Then the group would spend Saturday morning working in a local food bank along with another youth group.

Everything seemed to be in great shape. The young people were committed and excited. A local TV station picked up on the event, and ran a feature on Friday morning about how the young people had collected pledges for the 30-hour famine and how they would work in the food bank.

But no one showed up, and the adult leaders don't know why. "Last year what was popular isn't this year," lamented a frustrated youth leader. "We are trying to figure out why it suddenly petered out."

It is easy to become disenchanted with the prospects for youth service and giving when major events don't go as planned. A long-term perspective is an important reminder that each event or activity, though important, will not make or break a focus on nurturing generosity. Rather, it can become an opportunity for reflection, refinement, and refocusing in light of the overall commitment.


### SHIFT 3:
### FROM CONSUMERS OF SERVICES TO RESOURCES

One barrier to full engagement of young people in giving and serving is that, too often, they are viewed primarily as consumers or recipients of services within the congregation not as resources to others. Congregations focus on how they can "serve" youth, "meet young people's needs," "attract young people"—all of which can assume young people are the receivers, not the givers. The Rev. Dean Feldmeyer, a United Methodist pastor, put the challenge this way: "We're constantly in competition with the consumer culture. ... But we really can't compete. ... The goal is to help young people begin to see themselves not as consumers of religion and the church, but as practitioners of the faith."[25]

Silvia Blitzer Golombek, founder of Kids in Action in Washington, D.C., says she believes that the youth-as-consumers bias is deep and widespread in this culture. "Political science, anthropology, sociology, and education have all been influenced by the notion that children are not full-fledged individuals," she writes. "These fields often reflect the belief that children are empty vessels into which society pours its cultural values and norms of conduct—a process that turns children into adults, the 'proper' status to actively participate in today's world." She goes on to call for replacing "society's present attitude toward children with one that sees them as able, productive individuals who are part of society and whose voice needs to be heard"[26]

Until congregations begin to recognize that young people can and do make valuable contributions of both time and money, it is unlikely that young people will be authentically invited and challenged to develop the practices of generosity. Furthermore, they will not discover their own capacity to make a difference unless they have meaningful opportunities to do so.

Part of recognizing young people as resources is tapping into their own gifts, talents, and interests. At the Netarts Friends Church in Tillamook, Oregon, the Rev. Matthew York Lacy, the youth pastor, pays close attention to each young person's gifts, interests, and talents. "If you see them taking an interest in service, then you do that. If you see them [having] some ability in acting, you do that," he says. "As facilitators for Christ, we should be working with the gifts that God has given us and really working with those."

Lacy is aware that young people really like high-tech games like laser tag, but that doesn't mean one should create a youth program around laser tag. "I'm not saying cater to the youth," he said. Instead, it's better to know the young people as individuals, he suggested, to realize what they have to offer, and to understand what they're interested in rather than trying to plug them into an existing program that others think is good for them.

His group once went into Portland, Oregon, for its mission trip instead of going to Mexico. Some of the young people were upset because they were looking forward to having an adventure in another country. But Lacy discerned that some of the young people were being called to serve those in Portland. "It's all about having a positive relationship with Jesus so we can hear his leading so we know where we're supposed to be going."

## SHIFT 4:
## FROM PROGRAMS TOWARD RELATIONSHIPS

At Tree of Life Missionary Baptist Church in Gary, Indiana, "Young people are involved in every aspect of our ministry," said Pastor Cato Brooks, Jr. "They are teaching, singing in the choir, mentoring, preaching, working in the community. . . . We teach our young people; we don't have them play kiddie games." This active involvement connects them with many adults in the congregation, who actively nurture young people. As Deion, 16, reported, "At church you know someone will pick you up if you need it, and there is always a hand on your back, and you always feel it there."[27]

At Tree of Life young people have been integrated throughout the life of the congregation, and relationships have become the context for growth, learning, and involvement. That approach stands in contrast to the dominant model of youth work, defined by a series of programs, events, and packaged curricula[28]—youth group meetings, religious education classes, summer camp, service or social action projects, choir, and so forth. Each of these activities can provide structures and opportunities for participation, relationship building, faith nurture, skill building, and other goals. However, too often programs and activities become the ends, not the means. A guide for youth programs from the Union of American Hebrew Congregation states: "At the heart of a youth-friendly congregation is a commitment to the building of caring relationships. Programs and activities have their place, but the congregation will never reach its full potential for youth service unless it pays attention to nurturing caring relationships—the essence of community—between youth and their parents, youth and other youth, and youth and other adults."[29]

Congregations lose much of their potential impact when they rely too heavily on programs, curricula, and activities for nurturing the values of caring and generosity. As highlighted in numerous ways in the studies summarized earlier in this chapter, a commitment to generosity is nurtured primarily through relationships. Furthermore, relationships play a critical role for young people in moving from childhood through adolescence and into adulthood. As Kenda Creasy Dean and Ron Foster write:

> Significant relationships are the "blankies" youth carry with them to mediate their passage from the familiar territory of the primary family into the public and sometimes scary world of adulthood. In these relationships, adolescents discover who they are through the eyes of trusted others. . . . In the protected space of friendship, teens may safely try on various selves until they find one that fits. Of particular importance to adolescents is a friendship with an adult who sees in them potential they do not necessarily see in themselves.[30]

To be sure, there has been an emphasis in recent years on the importance of relationships in youth work—called "relational ministry" in Christian settings. However, too often the emphasis is on building relationships between young people and a small group of adult leaders. The challenge is to build on that emphasis and focus on discovering how young people can develop meaningful relationships with many people of all ages within the congregation and in the community. For it is through those relationships that young people not only experience care and generosity (which they can then pass on to others), but also where they can be invited, challenged, motivated, and equipped to give and serve.

Relationships are also an important component of connecting to families. Instead of a traditional family education component, Mount Zion Temple in St. Paul, Minnesota, has established a mentoring program for families as part of its bar and bat mitzvah preparation. According to Rabbi Adam Stock Spilker, every family with a sixth grader is paired with the family of an older student. Not only does this approach create a sense of community, but it also gives families someone they can call to ask questions. The mentor family invites the mentee family for a Shabbat dinner, then follows up with phone calls at particular times during the process. At the end of the year, the families get together for debriefing and thinking about the next year.

### SHIFT 5:
### FROM FRAGMENTED PROGRAMS TOWARD AN INTEGRATED VISION

The widespread tendency to focus on programs, activities, and curricula can easily lead to a patchwork of programs and activities that are unconnected and are offered either "to give kids something to do" or "because we've always had them." One Search Institute study of 500 religious youth workers found that only 43 percent had a clear mission statement for their youth program."[31] This lack of focus surely affects congregations' intentions to nurture generosity, and it also can make it difficult to sustain a long-term focus or vision.

Having an integrated, long-term vision for nurturing generosity among young people is a critical shift for congregations. Such a vision might recognize several dimensions:

• That the total culture of the congregation and a wide array of relationships and role models across generations can help to nurture in young people a commitment to giving and serving. (That potential is difficult to realize, however, when congregations segregate the "youth group" from other areas of congregational life. As Dean and Foster write: "The problem, we have discovered after a hundred years of youth groups, is that the youth group is notoriously unreliable for fostering ongoing faith." They note that youth groups create "an environment in which youth . . . had only marginal contact with the rest of the body of Christ.")[32]

- That the developmental path through childhood and adolescence underscores the importance of planting seeds early and seeking to nurture and cultivate generosity in age-responsive ways throughout the first two decades of life. Such a perspective begins to break down isolation between age-specific program areas, recognizing that lessons, relationships, experiences, and practices introduced early in life lay the foundation for later experiences and opportunities.

- That many aspects of congregational, family, and community life shape young people's generosity, not just "youth programming." A broader vision recognizes the potential of all these influences as resources and allies, then begins to discover how to increase the likelihood that these influences have a positive impact.

- That a particular experience in giving and serving is part of a long-term process of cultivating a habit of giving and serving. Thus, while it may be important to encourage young people to give to a particular cause or need, it's even more important, in the long run, to build on those one-time experiences so that young people have consistent, ongoing opportunities to give and serve.

This kind of long-term perspective and vision is clearly evident at Temple Emanu-El in Dallas. According to Judi Ratner, the synagogue's youth director, program leaders ask this question about first graders: What do we want them to be when they graduate from high school? Then they plan the program for all ages with that focus and developmental needs in mind. "I look at the whole thing as a trajectory, and ask how you build bridges across the groups," Ratner explained.

In first to fifth grades, the program offers fun activities for children three times a year, Ratner says, "to create fellowship and a sense of Jewish continuity." This time is important for forming community because otherwise the children—who attend many different schools—never really get to know each other or form strong friendships.

In seventh and eighth grades, more energy is put into keeping the young people interested and excited to be involved in their bar or bat mitzvah. Then by ninth grade, the youth program involves a lot of service projects, special outings and retreats, Jewish content, and leadership development.[33] The cumulative impact of this approach is that, by the end of high school, young people have developed deep bonds to the synagogue and commitments to making a difference and contributing through their synagogue.

There are, of course, many comprehensive, integrated approaches to youth work. Perhaps one of the more well developed is the model presented in the National Conference of Catholic Bishops' pastoral letter on youth ministry, Renewing the Vision. This document identifies seven themes of a comprehensive vision:

- *Developmental appropriateness* that "builds upon the growth nurtured in childhood and provides a foundation for continued growth in young adulthood"
- *Family-friendly* approaches that incorporate a family perspective into all programs and activities, recognizing the home as "the primary educators of faith and virtues"
- *Intergenerational* engagement that cultivates meaningful involvement in congregational life and that builds relationships across generations
- *Multicultural* emphases that celebrate the cultural heritages of the participating young people while also teaching about other heritages, traditions, values, and rituals in ways that help "young people learn about, understand, and appreciate people with backgrounds different from their own"
- *Community-wide collaboration* that allows the congregation to engage in public issues and build partnerships to improve the well-being of all young people
- Leadership that involves a variety of youth and adults
- Flexible and adaptable programming that addresses "the changing needs and life situations of today's young people and their family within a particular community"[34]

## SHIFT 6:
### FROM ISOLATION TOWARD CONNECTIONS

Just as a comprehensive perspective within a congregation seeks to maximize the impact of multiple areas of congregational life, it's also important to recognize, honor, and link with others outside the congregation who can influence giving and serving.

Young people have many opportunities to learn and practice generosity; they don't necessarily have to be involved in a congregation-sponsored service project or giving initiative to be generous. As a faith community, the congregation can celebrate all acts of generosity and offer young people opportunities to reflect on, interpret, and find meaning in all of their life experiences.

Consider the recent emphasis in public schools on both service-learning and financial literacy. How can congregations tap into those opportunities for young people? It could be as simple as providing opportunities for young people to reflect on their school experiences through the lens of faith. Or it could involve supplementing financial education coursework (in home economics, for example) with a discussion of the place of giving or sharing in responsible money management. Or the connections could involve cooperation on particular projects. Regardless of the approach, finding ways to affirm and reinforce the many opportunities young people have to give and serve not only reduces the pressure on congregations to do it all; it also helps young people integrate the many dimensions of their own lives.

## SHIFT 7:
### FROM A FEW YOUNG PEOPLE TOWARD ALL

Increased recognition is needed for the fact that young people are resources for congregations and communities. An even greater need is to recognize that all young people—regardless of economic status, ability, or vulnerability and risk—have capacity for generosity through giving and serving. Too often, opportunities to contribute are limited (often unintentionally) to middle- and upper-class youth. Those from lower income levels are stereotyped as not having enough to be able to "give back." In her comprehensive look at the state of religious youth work, Kenda Creasy Dean critiques the scope of service opportunities for youth:

Much of the community service which has benefited religious youth organizations has been limited to white, middle-class teenagers seeking confrontation with an economically disadvantaged sector of society, a decidedly lopsided vision of community service that borders precariously on paternalism. . . . Conscious efforts to foster mutuality between cultures involved in service projects . . . are important vehicles for including vulnerable populations in the empowering experience of giving.[35]

Pastor Joseph Bailey of Box Elder, Montana, struggles with the cultural bias whenever he tries to use print or video resources on youth service. "One of the most terrible things is for our kids [on the reservation] to open up a book about service projects and all the kids in there are white, and they're all getting out of minivans, and there's a bunch of soccer moms around them, . . . and Dad's coming home in a suit. It would be nice to see some dads in there with braids and wearing a construction outfit."

On a broader level, the U.S. Department of Education found that low-income youth are much less likely to report performing community service than those with higher income levels. According to data from the 1992 follow-up survey of the National Education Longitudinal Study of 1988, only 30 percent of high school seniors with the lowest income levels reported performing community service, compared to 60 percent of young people with the highest income levels.[36]

The problem, suggests a report from the Children's Defense Fund, is that "disadvantaged youths are thought of as recipients of service, not givers." However, the report notes that engaging marginalized young people in service efforts "can play an instrumental role in reducing the chances of dropping out of school or other poor outcomes among participants. Given the proper guidance, direction, and supervision, young people respond well to the responsibility of service and sense the value of their efforts."[37]

These issues challenge congregations to examine how efforts to engage young people in giving and serving do or do not include those who are marginalized or who are assumed to need help, not to be contributors. Alphonso Wyatt of Allen Temple A.M.E. Church in Jamaica, Queens, New York, is blunt: "If we believe that giving is a good thing, then why would we withhold a good thing unless we believe that people won't give, or that they will steal, or that their brokenness is their fault?"

## SHIFT 8:
### FROM ASSUMED LEARNING TOWARD INTENTIONAL GROWTH

Virtually everyone agrees that growth and learning come through giving and serving. Much less common are opportunities for thoughtful reflection that help young people interpret and internalize their experiences in giving and serving. Even less common are concrete opportunities to reflect on service and giving in light of the language, writings, and traditions of faith.

Too often when young people engage in serving others or giving financially, the projects focus entirely on getting the job done, then moving on to the next thing, assuming that the youth have learned more about themselves, others, and their world. But that's not necessarily the case. As Catholic educator Thomas Groome has written: "It is often glibly asserted that all experience is educational. But this is not automatically true. Some experiences are miseducational and others are not educational at all because we do not attend deliberately and intentionally to what they could possibly teach us."[38]

One of the challenges that congregations face in integrating reflection into giving and serving experiences is, once again, the fragmentation and compartmentalization of congregational life. In many cases, youth social-action or service projects and giving efforts are planned with little connection to the congregation's religious education efforts. As a result, religious education misses the opportunity for experiential learning, and the social-action activities do not tap the resources and expertise of religious educators. Exacerbating the problem, most resources for youth service or social action in congregations focus on the how-tos of the service project ideas, with little or no attention to reflection.[39]

Reflection should be a strength of congregations, particularly in connecting acts of generosity with the traditions, beliefs, and practices of faith. Indeed, Rabbi Dennis Eisner of Hebrew Union College–Jewish Institute of Religion in Los Angeles contends that the central role of religious leaders is to help young people make those connections. "Our role as professionals and as rabbis and as educators is to put it into a Jewish context," he explained. "Why is it so important that we do this? What makes it a Jewish act? What makes it a godly act? And that becomes part of our responsibility: helping them understand that feeding the hungry is so much more than just a simple act—that it also has to do with honoring people."

Research in the field of service-learning clearly affirms the importance of reflection. For example, a five-year Search Institute study of the

National Service-Learning Initiative and the Generator Schools—efforts managed by the National Youth Leadership Council—found that young people are more likely to report positive outcomes when their service-learning experience includes reflection. Furthermore, when reflection is minimal or absent, undesirable results are seen. For example, young people who didn't reflect were more likely to develop negative views toward serving others.[40]

A focus on learning and reflection also speaks to the reality of silence in many congregations, particularly in Christian traditions, regarding money and giving. Congregations must strengthen, discover, or recover the language and culture that allow for open reflection and conversation about how young people and adults use their time and their money. Only then can they offer meaningful opportunities for internalizing the values, priorities, and practices of faith and generosity.

## Moving toward Future Possibilities

We began this chapter by looking at examples of what researchers have found to be important factors in nurturing generosity and caring in children and youth. That research, combined with reflection on the realities outlined in chapters 2 through 4, suggested eight culture shifts that begin to connect present realities with future possibilities, knowing that we can see glimpses of the latter in the stories of congregations that are already on this journey. The eight culture shifts begin to offer an alternative vision of congregations in which nurturing generosity is embedded throughout congregational life. At one level, this vision is daunting, since, in many instances, there is so much to be done. At the same time, the research on generosity and the experiences of congregations suggest concrete ways that congregations can continue the journey toward being communities of faith where the practices of generosity become a way of life for young people.

# CHAPTER 6

# Creating a Culture of Generosity

To this point, we have examined the current state of giving and serving in congregations, some of the factors that contribute to lifelong generosity, and culture shifts needed for congregations to be more effective in nurturing generosity in young people. This chapter begins exploring what congregations can do to cultivate in young people a lifelong commitment to generosity.

Chapters 6 and 7 are built around a set of eight keys to giving and serving in congregations[1] (summarized in figure 10 on page 106). The first four keys (the focus of this chapter) emphasize creating a generous culture throughout a congregation. They deal with the commitments, traditions, norms, and climate of the congregation, particularly as they relate to giving and serving. The next four keys, discussed in chapter 7, focus on the practices of generosity—engaging young people in giving and serving, and involving families and the wider intergenerational community of faith as part of that process.

The eight keys are not listed in order of priority. Rather, they fit together to suggest a comprehensive (or ecological) view of a congregation that effectively addresses giving and serving with young people, as suggested in figure 1, chapter 1. Furthermore, the eight keys link together and reinforce each other. For example, key 3, "Connect to faith and traditions," clearly provides the framework for infusing the language and practices of faith into all the other keys. Similarly, key 5, "Provide opportunities for youth to practice giving," is shaped by family involvement (key 7), the congregation's commitment to others (key 1), and others. Thus, it is important not to think of each key in isolation, but as part of a larger whole.

# Figure 10

## Summary of Eight Keys to Nurturing Generosity

**Key #1: Commit to the well-being of others**—The congregation sees giving and serving as part of its commitment to its neighbors, community, nation, and world.
• The congregation has a clear commitment to meeting needs.
• The congregation's clergy and lay leaders show a commitment to giving and serving in their own lives.
• The congregation humanizes issues by introducing youth to the people behind the problems—and people who are finding solutions.
• The congregation encourages young people to think critically about their faith and the world.

**Key #2: Cherish children and youth**—The congregation values young people and helps them know that they are important members of the faith community.
• The congregation is a warm and welcoming place for children and youth.
• Young people are personally invited to participate, serve, give, and lead.
• Young people have useful roles in the congregation.
• Congregation leaders and members recognize and support the ways young people contribute to the congregation.
• The congregation has a comprehensive approach to child and youth nurturing and engagement in congregational life.

**Key #3: Connect to faith and traditions**—The congregation's commitments to giving and serving are grounded in its sacred texts, teachings, traditions, and identity.
• The congregation offers quality religious education experiences for all ages.
• All adults, youth, and children have opportunities to learn about giving and serving in their faith's sacred texts, teachings, theology, and traditions.
• Young people have opportunities to reflect on giving and serving within the context of their faith.
• Giving and serving are integrated with the congregation's rituals and traditions.

**Key #4: Establish norms and expectations**—Giving and serving are integral, ongoing emphases in congregational life.
• The congregation's leadership articulates a commitment to giving and serving for all ages throughout the year.
• People of all ages are expected to give and serve.
• Symbols and reminders of giving and serving are prominent in the congregation.
• Giving and serving are integrated into all areas of congregational life.
• Young people inspire the congregation to engage in giving and serving.

**Key #5: Provide opportunities for youth to practice giving**—The congregation encourages and supports young people's financial giving.
- The congregation offers guidance and support in making faithful, responsible choices about money.
- Young people are active decision makers in the giving process.
- Young people are encouraged and guided to plan their giving.
- Emphasis is placed on the habit of giving, not the amount given.
- Young people can see tangible results from their giving.
- Young people have opportunities to talk about and reflect on their financial giving.

**Key #6: Provide opportunities for youth to practice serving**—The congregation plans, encourages, and supports young people's involvement in serving others.
- Young people take an active leadership role in planning and leading service activities.
- Service experiences are thoughtfully planned to address real community needs as well as the growth and development of young people.
- Young people have ongoing opportunities to serve others.
- Young people have opportunities to reflect on their service involvement.
- Young people's acts of service are recognized, affirmed, and celebrated by the whole congregation.

**Key #7: Support families**—The congregation supports and equips parents in their efforts to encourage their children to give and serve.
- The congregation views parents as key partners in nurturing generosity in young people.
- The congregation integrates a family perspective into giving and serving activities.
- The congregation provides parents with support, education, and resources to inspire and equip them to encourage giving and serving in the home.
- The congregation offers opportunities for families to serve together.

**Key #8: Connect generations**—Opportunities for giving and serving build bridges between young people and other generations in the community of faith.
- All adults in the congregation understand their responsibility to nurture, guide, and care for young people.
- Young people have role models for giving and serving in the congregation.
- The congregation provides opportunities for all generations to give and serve together.

## BACKGROUND TO THE EIGHT KEYS

Much of the material we have reviewed for this book offers planning guide-lines for two concrete programs—one focused on giving (stewardship or *tzedakah*), and one on serving others (social action, missions, *tikkun olam*). In contrast, we offer here a congregationwide, systemic approach, which, we believe, more accurately responds to the complexity of congregational life and the dynamics of growing up with a commitment to generosity. Rare is the person who can point to a specific program that, by itself, cemented a lifelong commitment. For most people, that kind of commitment grows out of years of observation, experimentation, exploration, and reinforcement. While such an approach may frustrate those looking for a straightforward "generosity program," we believe that it offers much more promise for lasting change and commitment.

This conceptual framework seeks to integrate themes from at least four perspectives:

- Research on factors in the lives of young people and adults that con-tribute to shaping a life of generosity (see chapter 5)
- A scan of other research, as well as interviews with congregational leaders and other experts, that suggests "best practices" related to youth giving, youth service, and youth philanthropy
- A synthesis of current trends in congregation-based youth work
- The strength-based, holistic understanding of adolescent development that undergirds Search Institute's work on developmental assets and the building of developmentally attentive communities[2]

We see this framework as an important starting point for reflection and conversation within congregations and among those who serve congrega-tions and observe congregational life. Congregational leaders and other ex-perts who have reviewed it in various draft stages found it to be a useful tool for beginning to understand the complex dynamics of a focus on creat-ing a congregational culture in which generosity becomes a way of life. We encourage you to apply, test, adapt, and refine the framework—and share what you learn with us.[3]

Think of these eight keys as conversation starters that can help you see new possibilities and options. Few congregations will do everything included in the framework. However, by presenting a larger vision of con-gregational life, the keys may help you think about giving and serving from a fresh point of view.

## KEY 1: COMMIT TO THE WELL-BEING OF OTHERS

A commitment to the well-being of others is fundamental to a generous life and a generous community of faith. It speaks to a sense of social responsibility, social justice, caring and compassion, *tikkun olam*—repair of the world. It asks the question, What is the role of the community of faith (individually and corporately) in meeting the needs of others and in working for the "common good"?

Though expressed in a wide variety of ways, a commitment to addressing the needs of others through acts of compassion and justice is integral to the teachings of Jewish and Christian traditions.[4] However, that commitment is not always evident in the priorities and practices of congregations. Furthermore, even congregations with strong traditions of social responsibility may not always explicitly pass that commitment on to young people. They may believe that the young people should be served rather than serve, that young people will automatically pick up the commitment from the congregation's leaders, or that they will pick up the commitments when they become adults.

A commitment to others has different emphases, depending on traditions. An ongoing dialogue in the Jewish community, for example, concerns the balance between addressing specifically Jewish causes and tending to broader issues of social justice. "If you go back to the period between the Civil War and the Depression, there were a lot of immigrant Jews in America," explained Elliot Abrams, president of the Ethics and Public Policy Center in Washington, D.C. "The question then of what Jewish charity was for was very simple. Jewish charity was basically to help poor Jews. . . . But since World War II it has become really a great deal less relevant as Jews have come out of poverty. So there is a debate now. What do all these traditions tell you about your obligations outside the Jewish community?"[5]

That issue is concrete for the Jewish young people we interviewed. They tell of their experiences in service through a variety of Christian social service agencies in the city (such as staffing a homeless shelter on Christmas Eve). One young woman expressed her philosophy this way: "I am surprised how relatively comfortable I felt when I got to that shelter and realized it was a Christian shelter," she says. "It's like you're still doing something for the community, and . . . everybody needs it just as much."

Across traditions, a commitment to meeting the needs of others lays a foundation for giving and serving. Thus, this first key focuses on the importance of an articulated, shared vision and commitment—one that is shaped and shared with young people. This clear commitment and the example set by leaders set the direction and priority that giving and serving have in the congregation. This commitment has at least three dimensions:

*The congregation has a clear commitment to meeting needs.* A congregation's commitment to meeting needs in the world becomes visible in many ways. It may be a recurring theme in sermons and public gatherings. It may be evident in the budget or in service or social action projects, programs, and activities sponsored by the congregation or participated in by its members. It may be visible in the congregation's affiliations and the organizations it supports.

These commitments can take many forms around many issues, depending on the congregation's history, culture, and theological perspective. In their in-depth studies of how Christian churches engage in ministry in communities, Carl S. Dudley and Sally A. Johnson identified five basic congregational images that shaped the type of action they undertook. While the study was limited to Christian congregations, the findings seem relevant across the faith spectrum. Here, briefly, are the five types of congregations and the kinds of activities they are most likely to do in the community:

- *Pillar congregations* are like the stable pillars of a community that take responsibility for strengthening the whole. They can mobilize significant resources to meet needs, and they are most likely to support ongoing programs and initiatives.
- Often founded by immigrants, *pilgrim congregations* emphasize relationships, and congregational life binds them to one another and to their cultural heritage. While members don't think of themselves as activists, they are often involved in services of compassion aimed at long-term improvement in people's lives—the kind of hope that drew them to emigrate.
- *Survivor congregations* always seem to struggle, but they have surprising energy to address the problems they face, often in declining neighborhoods. The struggle creates a sense of unity that gives them strength to rally around crises in the community. Their experiences have taught them never to give up.
- *Prophet congregations* are the ones most ready to risk for their sense of calling and justice. These congregations tend to be impatient self-starters, and ready to make partnerships and coalitions with other congregations and agencies committed to the same cause.

- Finally, *servant congregations* respond primarily to individual needs. They are less inclined to get on board with the latest issue; rather, they offer steady, consistent service to address the needs around them.[6]

Allen A.M.E. Church in Jamaica, Queens, New York, is clearly a "pillar" congregation. Since its founding, said the Rev. Alphonso Wyatt, associate minister, this church has had "a tradition of community building, of economic development." The church's commitment is evident in the tremendous investment it has made in building the community infrastructure, supporting African-American colleges, building homes for the community, a school, and other activities and investments. "We have some very powerful home-grown lessons," Wyatt said. "Our job is to make sure it's harvested . . . that the young people really understand."

*The congregation's clergy and lay leaders show a commitment to giving and serving in their own lives.* A congregation's commitment to giving and serving, to attending to the welfare of others, is greatly enhanced through the example of active commitment set by its leaders, including young people who assume leadership roles with youth or in the whole congregation. As Michael Lerner writes, "Be what you want to teach."[7]

As noted in chapter 3, most youth workers, clergy, and other congregational leaders find it easier to demonstrate a commitment to serving others than to giving money. This discomfort may grow from the general unease with honest discussions about money. Or it may grow from the leaders' own economic realities, beliefs, and choices. Writing to Christian churches, Mark Vincent notes that "too many pastors feel inadequate to manage their own finances, let alone provide spiritual instruction about money." He contends that "pastors, elders, deacons, and other church leaders need to tell their life stories about money. They need to be offered healing, hope, and accountability when anger, fear, pain, and sin come to the surface. Once they are renewed, they need to lead church members in a similar experience.[8]

*The congregation humanizes issues by introducing youth to the people behind the problems—and people who are finding solutions.* Exposing young people to issues in the world—and showing that they can made a difference in addressing those issues—is at the heart of Danny Siegel's message within the Jewish community. He believes that exposing young people to social issues and injustices unleashes their creativity and passion. "You walk them to a Dumpster and say, 'There are 300 doughnuts in here from Dunkin' Donuts.' And they are going to simply say, 'This is not right,' and they are going to find a way to donate them to the shelters." He concluded: "I'm fascinated by kids' power."

But Siegel doesn't expose young people to issues by holding lectures on pressing social problems or writing topical curricula. Rather, he introduces youth and adults to "*mitzvah* heroes"—ordinary kids and adults who have done extraordinary things to help to heal the world. He often tells stories of these heroes, both contemporary and historical.[9] But his favorite approach is to bring the heroes with him when he goes to speak at schools, colleges, congregations, and conventions across the country.

Support for Siegel's personalized approach emerged in the Church and Community Ministry project, led by Carl S. Dudley of Hartford Seminary in Connecticut. The project worked with 40 congregations of a variety of denominations, cultures, and socioeconomic levels to launch social ministries in the community. In the process, the researchers learned that some early assumptions were not accurate. Dudley writes:

> Church groups wanted ministry with people they could name in their communities, who had problems and needed assistance. Congregations did not think about 'issues,' but about their friends and neighbors, the strengths of real people—who have problems that outsiders call issues. . . . Naming people has the power to motivate congregational effort. . . . As relational institutions, congregations care about individual people. Naming people helps.[10]

Humanizing and personalizing the issues can have an immediate, significant impact on young people. Mary Kohlsdorff of Ankeny (Iowa) Presbyterian Church told of an experience with her youth group on a Sunday night. The morning sermon had focused on helping people incorporate a sense of service into everyday life. So Kohlsdorff decided to take the message to the senior high youth group, which usually ordered pizza for the meeting (with each person bringing $3). "Instead of ordering pizza," she suggested, "let's pool our money and run up to the grocery store and fix something that's pretty cheap." The leftover money, she said, could be used to buy needed towels, shampoo, or other supplies for the local homeless shelter.

"For a minute they just kind of looked at me like, 'You're kidding me.' . . . Then I read a letter that one of the homeless people had written. . . . He had a master's degree in engineering, but he had ended up being homeless."

Kohlsdorff didn't pressure the young people any more, offering to order the pizza if that was their preference. Then they started saying, "Let's just make macaroni and cheese, because we can probably feed all of us for $2. . . . So we divided up. Some went to get the macaroni and cheese, and the rest of us went to Wal-Mart and bought the supplies."

Another way to expose young people to issues and the people behind the issues is to take them to places where they experience issues first-hand. Alphonso Wyatt tells of a program that exposes young people from the Bronx and Harlem to issues they might otherwise ignore. For example, they went to hospitals "where they changed and held babies born addicted to drugs. That really changed the perspective of both the young men and the young women," he said.

In addition to introducing young people to those who are affected by issues and those who are actively working to address them, congregations can also humanize global issues through simulations and other similar experiential activities. For example, as part of a community-wide, interfaith youth initiative, Jewish and Christian congregations in Durham, North Carolina, sponsored a hunger banquet for youth. This type of event simulates the world's uneven food distribution, with a few people being served bountiful feasts while most receive much less—or almost nothing. After this simulated learning experience, the youth participated in a CROP Walk to raise money for the hungry in their community, the nation, and the world.

*The congregation encourages young people to think critically about their faith and the world.* In personalizing issues and needs, it's important that young people be exposed to people and issues that are unfamiliar—and have opportunities to reflect on these encounters. This reflective process helps guide youth to recognize and reflect on systemic issues that underlie individual crises, problems, or needs.

In a study of adult volunteers, Robert Wuthnow found that "many of the volunteers we spoke with remained shielded from deeper injustices. Their compassion had focused too much on people like themselves, or they saw the people they helped only as individuals, not as symptoms of some larger problem in American society. When they thought about injustice, the notion was therefore more distant, less charged with emotion, like a concept they had read about but not experienced directly."[11]

While there is value in classes and curricula that introduce young people to their faith responsibility in the world, the more powerful learning comes when young people have opportunities to reflect on their faith and social issues within the context of concrete experiences of giving or serving. These connections can be made in many creative ways.

For example, Rabbi Neal Gold of New Brunswick, New Jersey, once invited representatives from Canine Companions for Independence, which provides guide dogs for the blind. "The kids were enthralled," he reported. In the process, he helped the young people begin to recognize the Jewish vocabulary and approach to caring and justice, and understand "what's Jewish about the whole concept of opening up somebody's world—for a person with disabilities."

## Key 2: Cherish Children and Youth

Children and youth learn how to care for and value others when they are cared for and valued themselves. And they're more likely to give and serve when they believe their contribution is useful and meaningful. These experiences help young people bond to and value the congregation. Congregations that value young people have the potential to become communities in which young people generously share their time, talents, and treasures with those close to them and those they do not know.

Research by Dean Hoge of Catholic University found that an indirect but important influence on lifelong giving among adults was a sense of being committed to their congregation. Furthermore, that commitment usually had its roots in adolescence. "[Generous adults] all tell you stories about youth ministry especially," he explained, "about going on retreats, about going on any type of event in which there was bonding. They all tell stories about the wonderful people who influenced them when they were [adolescents]. . . . Those people end up being the backbone of the church."

Being cherished, cared for, and valued are important elements in bonding to the congregation. And while close relationships with peers and with the handful of adult leaders directly involved in youth programming are important, this key suggests the importance of a broader sense of connection and inclusion of children and youth within congregational life. We propose that the following five elements are essential building blocks for cultivating a congregation that cherishes its young people.

*The congregation is a warm and welcoming place for children and youth.* If, as the research shows, being connected to a congregation increases the likelihood that youth and adults will give and serve, then helping young people feel warm and welcome in the congregation is a high priority. Indeed, a Search Institute study of five mainline Protestant Christian denominations found that "a warm climate" has an important influence on people's loyalty to their congregation.[12]

In his in-depth interviews with adults about their religious experiences as children and youth, Robert Wuthnow found that some of the most powerful memories of their congregations were about a sense of community. He writes:

> Although people remember the activities and the physical space in which they attended services, it is the sense of *belonging* that clearly matters most. They look back with fondness at the cousins and best friends with whom they attended services, at the fact that church or synagogue was where they saw members of their extended family, and at teachers who made them feel special. When this sense of community is lacking, people who have nevertheless attended regularly still feel in retrospect that religion was difficult to understand and was somehow removed from the rest of their life.[13]

Youth workers note that feeling welcomed is a precursor to young people' becoming engaged in serving and giving. As Alan Stock Spilker of Mount Zion Temple in St. Paul, Minnesota, says, "If they are not already connected with friendships, it's hard to convince them to try out something, when they could do something else with their friends they already have." Many congregations face the additional challenge that young people attend different schools and don't see each other day to day. "If they miss one event," Spilker says, "then they might see each other . . . once every two months, if at all."

Sometimes it can be hard to capture what congregations do that help young people feel welcomed. But the kids know it when they experience it. A Baptist youth described some experiences that make her feel valued: "People come up to me after church and say, 'I am so glad to see that you are sitting next to us in church,' and, 'I love to see you around here.' Especially people like older citizens come up to me and start talking about how they love to see us around the church. I think it's important to them to see their kids grow up."

Young people's perceptions of warmth and friendliness may vary considerably, depending on their level of involvement in the congregation.

A Search Institute study of youth in one Protestant denomination found that 57 percent of young people who are active leaders or volunteers in the congregation and 42 percent of regular attenders believe the congregation has a warm, welcoming, and friendly climate. In contrast, only 24 percent of the inactive feel this way.[14] Thus, if a congregation is to engage young people in serving and giving, then attention must be paid to discovering how best to reach out and include the young people who feel like peripheral "outsiders" in the congregation or youth group.

Another important variable to consider in ensuring that all young people feel welcomed is age. Most faith traditions see a dramatic decrease in youth involvement between younger and older adolescents.[15] This trend suggests both the importance of guiding young people through the critical transition from younger to older adolescence (around ages 13 to 15) and the importance of discovering what, if anything, the congregation can do to maintain a connection with older youth—rather than simply shutting down most programming for older youth because of a lack of participation.

*Young people are personally invited to participate, serve, give, and lead.* One way to help young people feel valued and valuable is to ask them to contribute—not through mass mailings, but through personal invitations: "I'm wondering if you would like to _____, because I know you are committed to _____."

Being invited to lead, give, and serve is a critical element in engaging young people. Indeed, in its report on youth giving and serving, Independent Sector noted that "volunteers are not made, but asked." This research found that 93 percent of young people who were asked to volunteer by someone close to them did volunteer. In contrast, only 24 percent of those volunteered who were not personally asked. Unfortunately, only half of the young people surveyed were ever invited to volunteer.[16] When congregations complain that young people won't do anything, a question needs to be asked: Did you invite them? And if you did, did you invite them to do something that was meaningful for them?

Personal invitations require extra effort. Heidi Tarshish of Temple Israel in Minneapolis believes that a personal invitation is the key. "Personalizing everything is extremely important," she said. "If I have someone who's not registered, I call them and say: 'I want you here, you're important. How can I help to get you here? What do you need from me?' I think that you have to go the extra step. . . . They need to know someone cares and if they're not there, they are going to be missed. Even if our kids miss one program, we send a note home. . . . It's not like a punishment, the kids know that we don't want you to feel out of the loop of things, we want you to feel included, part of the community."

*Young people have useful roles in the congregation.* Congregations that effectively engage youth in giving and serving recognize young people consistently as a resource and, as a result, give them meaningful, useful roles in the congregation.

Joseph Bailey, who serves a church on the Rocky Boy Reservation in Montana, sees this attitude as the foundation for his congregation's youth efforts. "Our youth do everything around here. We encourage [youth] to do just about everything in the context of the congregation. I'm just as apt to call a young person up who's 12 to be my communion assistant as I am a 60-year-old person. Nobody looks at that funny anymore. They used to when I started doing it. . . . And so from the very start, I assume our youth members are full members of the congregation. They're not youth members, they're members, and they have the rights and the responsibilities that go with that."

Young people are integrated throughout the leadership at Anshei Emeth Memorial Congregation in New Brunswick, New Jersey. Not only do youth representatives sit on the temple's *tzedakah* committee, reported Rabbi Neal Gold, but they also are involved on the religious school committee and the temple's board of trustees. In addition, the high school youth have an elected board that plans and leads youth activities.

"We try to drill into their heads," Gold said, "that bar mitzvah isn't a graduation. . . . It's just the beginning of things." He wants young people to understand that "now I am ready to be a Jewishly responsible adult. And now I'm really ready to begin being responsible for my own Jewish education and being responsible to my community."

*Congregation leaders and members recognize and support the ways young people contribute to the congregation.* Young people's meaningful participation in the congregation will not lead to a sense of being cherished if those contributions are not supported and recognized. The support helps to ensure that young people are successful in their efforts. The recognition reinforces their involvement and helps them see its significance, encouraging them to continue and deepen their commitments.

A lack of support or recognition can be quite detrimental to young people. James P. Wind told of a time when his teenage daughter came home frustrated from a meeting about the congregation's youth group. "The plain message was that no adult seems to have enough time to give this," Wind recalled. He said he worries about how young people interpret those experiences. "If no one is interested in me," he suggested, "that sends a message that I'm probably not worth all that much and don't have that much to contribute."

Congregations have many ways to recognize young people for their contributions. Some congregations highlight youth service experiences (particularly extended work trips) in worship services and other publicity. Temple Israel in Minneapolis regularly recognizes young people for their efforts in the community through the temple's newsletter. "We call them mitzvah heroes," said Heidi Tarshish, who works with middle-school youth. Then at the end of the year, "there is a ceremony during a Friday night service where students in all areas of participation at this congregation are recognized and applauded."

*The congregation has a comprehensive approach to child and youth nurture and engagement in congregational life.* To this point, we have emphasized the relational and informal dimensions to cherishing young people. In addition, though, congregations also express their esteem for youth by addressing the range of their spiritual, physical, emotional, social, and intellectual needs. As a planning guide for Jewish youth workers puts it, "In a comprehensive youth program, all of a congregation's programs and services for youth (actual and potential) are viewed as one whole—like a large puzzle, where all of the pieces fit together in such a way that all of the congregation's youth are in the picture."[17]

A comprehensive approach emphasizes giving and serving within the larger context of the congregation's overarching goals and priorities for the faith nurture, healthy development, and identity formation of young people. In the process, all aspects of the congregation's work with children and youth—from education to worship to social activities—can become resources for nurturing generosity.

Many models for a comprehensive approach have been developed and published.[18] It should be noted, however, that most models focus primarily, if not exclusively, on work with adolescents or with children—rarely both. In addition, few comprehensive models in Christian traditions emphasize financial giving. Thus, most models need to be adapted to integrate a strong focus on giving and serving. However, the existing resources offer basic frameworks upon which to build an overall vision, goals, and strategies for engaging young people in congregational life throughout childhood and adolescence, recognizing the unique developmental phases, needs, and growth throughout that development process.

## KEY 3: CONNECT TO FAITH AND TRADITIONS

Many segments of society value the nurturing of generosity in young people. Indeed, key elements of U.S. society rely on voluntary action, civic engagement, philanthropic giving, and other acts of generosity. Indeed, as noted earlier, many institutions such as public schools increasingly seek to engage young people in service to others; congregations clearly do not have an exclusive role. Adding to the challenge, Robert Wuthnow reports that a declining proportion of Americans sees a strong connection between religion and generosity. His survey of American adults found that "only 30 percent of the public thought religious people are generally more compassionate than those with no religious convictions."[19] In short, people may be less and less likely to tap their faith tradition as the source of motivation and sustenance for their giving and serving.

This trend is also evident with young people. Indeed, many religious young people do not seem to ground their generosity in their faith tradition. As Eileen Campbell-Reed put it, "I do think there are these groups who [serve others], but I think they struggle to connect: What does that have to do with Jesus? What does that have to do with my faith?"

Sometimes young people have only vague notions of the faith roots of their involvement. Asked where he learned about giving and serving, one youth said, "Just random places in the Bible. I forget where it is now, but it's, yeah, in the Bible, and just along the way I learned about it."

And yet, if tapped, the rich traditions, writings, and tenets of faith can inspire and guide teenagers toward a life of generosity. Even more important, however, is to remember that acts of generosity are integral to a broader faith commitment and life of faith. Thus, this key to nurturing generosity in young people has two dimensions, both of which are critical in nurturing habits of giving and serving:

- A general emphasis on nurturing a life-shaping, identity-forming faith
- A specific emphasis on tying giving and serving to the faith tradition

The general emphasis on nurturing faith recognizes that giving and serving are a response of faith. Furthermore, research shows that generosity follows faithfulness. Sociologist Dean Hoge concludes in a major study of giving patterns among Christian adults: "People more strongly committed to God and God's promise give more."[20] Similarly, researchers in the Jewish community have found that "a stronger sense of religious identity does indeed increase . . . participation in both giving time and monetary contributions to Jewish philanthropies."[21] Other efforts—special appeals, creative publicity, offering envelopes—may help, but they won't compensate for a faith or religious identity that is stagnant.

The more specific emphasis that ties serving and giving to the faith tradition highlights the importance of passing on that tradition's values and customs regarding giving and serving. The congregation's commitment to nurturing giving and serving needs to be grounded in its sacred texts, teachings, and traditions in the following ways:

*The congregation offers quality religious education experiences for all ages.* A high-quality religious education program lays a foundation for nurturing faith throughout the congregation. Although some people automatically equate "religious education" with children, the intention here is to emphasize ongoing opportunities for faith and identity formation and growth throughout childhood, adolescence, and adulthood.

In its major study of congregations in six Protestant denominations in 1990, Search Institute found that one of the two strongest correlates of high faith maturity is lifetime involvement in Christian education. (For youth, the other strongest correlate is family religiosity; for adults, it is lifetime church involvement.)[22] Thus, if a life of generosity grows out of a strong, mature faith, then a priority should be placed on forming and sustaining that faith throughout life. This task can be accomplished through ongoing engagement of youth in study, dialogue, and other forms of faith formation and religious identity development.

While a focus on children seems obvious (since childhood experiences lay the foundation for faith formation in adolescence), some may wonder about the inclusion of an emphasis on adult faith and identity formation in a framework focused on youth. Two important factors lie behind this choice. First, it is vital that parents and other adults also have opportunities to grow in their own faith and identity because of their influence in young people's lives. Second, it is difficult to keep young people interested and engaged in faith-shaping activities through high school when they perceive that religious education and faith formation are activities for children, not adults. Indeed, there is some evidence that denominations that emphasize and maintain a stronger tradition of lifelong learning are more effective in keeping young people engaged throughout high school.[23]

*All adults, youth, and children have opportunities to learn about giving and serving in their faith's sacred texts, teachings, theology, and traditions.* If (as was suggested in chapters 3 and 4) one of the barriers to nurturing generosity in young people is a gap in explicit connections to the congregation's faith traditions, then an important task is to develop the discipline and language to talk about giving and serving from a faith perspective. Robert Wuthnow says in reference to financial giving, "The traditions do make a difference, and yet . . . people often don't know what's in the traditions, and they haven't heard very clear preaching that connects to their giving."

Many of the people interviewed noted the importance of using faith-specific language with young people. "I would never use in front of the kids words like social service, community service, volunteer [service], stuff like that," said Rabbi Neal Gold. "I try to use religious language around them." Presbyterian Mary Kohlsdorff voiced a similar perspective. "I think it's important to be able to back everything up biblically," she said. "It really helps when you feel [that] you're following what the Bible is telling you to do."

In addition to addressing the specific issue of language, congregations can help the traditions and texts come to life for young people. All Saints Lutheran Church in Cottage Grove, Minnesota, brought to life Jesus' parable of the talents (Matt. 25:14-30) for all youth and adult members. Each member was given ten dollars in the worship service one week and told to use it wisely. Two months later, the congregation got back all of the $2,600 it dispersed, plus about $3,000 more, which members accumulated by using their time, talents, and treasures wisely. For example, 16-year-old Sarah Schille and her father used the money to buy supplies to make bird feeders—which they then sold to raise money. "We quickly saw generosity breeding generosity," said Pastor Rolf Olson.[24]

The importance of connecting giving and serving to the faith traditions points to a potentially important role for pastors, rabbis, and other theologically trained leaders. Rabbi Adam Stock Spilker said that his extensive investment in studying the texts and traditions helps him to find valuable connections for youth and to identify effective ways to communicate. He points to the "ease with which I can throw out the information and make it fun and interesting and something that they can engage in instead of saying, 'Okay, now we need to open our book and find out the Jewish voice on this topic.' . . . It's always just a part of our dialogue."

*Young people have opportunities to reflect on giving and serving within the context of their faith.* Learning about one's faith traditions doesn't have to happen through a printed curriculum or in a classroom. In fact, the most effective learning is likely to happen through reflection on real-life experiences of giving and serving. Reflection provides the opportunity for young people to find meaning in their giving and serving experiences as they work through their experiences and feelings in juxtaposition with their faith and contemporary issues.

Wendy Schwartz of Beth Jacob Congregation in Mendota Heights, Minnesota, weaves learning into a wide range of social action projects. "A lot of what [youth] do has a textual connection," she said, "whether they study the text independently on a Saturday afternoon, or whether it's part of the program." She offered some examples: "They went to the zoo one time and they had someone come and speak about Jewish values in relation to taking care of animals. . . . When we did the adopt-the-river, it wasn't just, 'go pick up the garbage,' but they learned about the Jewish values involved with it and what the text says about caring for the land."

Such reflection can take many forms and take place in many settings. It can be highly structured as part of a well-designed service-learning project. It can occur in religious education settings in which young people are asked to reflect on prior experiences in giving and serving. Such dialog will inevitably enrich the lessons and curriculum.

*Giving and serving are integrated with the congregation's rituals and traditions.* The religious dimensions of giving and serving are most evident and powerful when these actions are part of the congregation's worship, rituals, festivals, and other traditions. Yet, when it comes to financial giving, some Christian congregations have either downplayed or abandoned one of the central acts of giving within the Christian tradition: the offering. "Apparently," writes Mark Vincent of the Giving Project, "the offering is not viewed as an integral part of worship." He continues:

> Receiving an offering is not a necessary evil. It is a time for God's people to declare their sole allegiance to, and sole dependence on, their Maker. Receiving an offering allows the entire congregation to participate in worship. It is a weekly opportunity to declare love for God, to express appreciation for the blessings of God, and to hear yet again what Christians believe about money. Instead of despairing of what to do with the offering, we need to claim the opportunity![25]

In contrast, *tzedakah* is an integral part of Jewish ritual life, both within the congregation and in the home. In her exploration of the Jewish philanthropic tradition, philanthropy expert Anita H. Plotinsky argues that "philanthropic behavior is learned by doing through lived traditions and customs." She shows how giving is an integral part of all major holidays and festivals, including the High Holy Days, which have "the three-fold theme of *teshuva*, *tefilah*, and *tzedakah*, or repentance, prayer, and charity. . . . The ten days surrounding the High Holy Days are regarded as an appropriate time both for contributions to charitable causes and for acts of kindness toward others."[26] She also describes how generosity is embedded in life-cycle events (including birth, marriage, and death) as well as rituals of everyday life (through practices such as *tzedakah* boxes).

Both Jewish and Christian congregations can find creative, meaningful ways to integrate giving and serving with worship and other traditions. Congregation Kehilath Jeshrun in New York City has a tradition of asking everyone—"every man, woman, boy, girl"—to bring one or more packages of food to services at the beginning of Yom Kippur. "We have these big barrels right in the entrance of the synagogue, in the entrance lobby, and people come in and deposit their bags or items into these big barrels," said the synagogue's executive director, Robert Leifert.

## Key 4: Establish Norms and Expectations

A wide range of research has shown that a social norm—"a standard or rule that is accepted by members of the group"[27]—can play a powerful role in shaping people's behaviors across a wide range of situations. Among young people, for example, those who inaccurately believe that sexual intercourse or smoking is the norm for teenagers are more likely to engage in those behaviors.[28]

Social norms not only shape negative behaviors; they can also encourage or reinforce positive behaviors (such as recycling). Indeed, the growing involvement of young people in service can create a new norm that both makes this positive activity appealing and also attaches some negative consequences (in terms of isolation or stigma) to not being involved.

For many religious communities, giving and serving have been normative—just what's expected. And while that is still true in some traditions and some congregations, too often there is no expectation for young people to give or serve, nor any consequences associated with doing so (or not doing so). Indeed, in some congregations, the norm in relation to giving is just the opposite. As a leader put it: "We would need permission to [ask youth to give]. . . . We don't ask for money often here, so we might be a little timid to go down and ask . . . the youth flat out, 'Do you know that you need to start giving?'"

In his work with Christian congregations, Mark Vincent sees reshaping norms as a vital part of his efforts. When congregations begin reshaping patterns, he said, "so much of the stuff is going on behind the scenes, and it fits so much into what a congregation would normally be doing." The difference, though, is that "you are getting more intentional about it. . . . It's fairly innocuous, as far as the work, but the results are quite extensive." His hope in working with congregations is that the attitude of giving is so integrated with the congregation's own self-understanding that "you just can't escape it."

Leadership, expectations, symbols, and integration throughout the congregation all play a role in creating (or re-creating) a norm within the congregation that encourages young people to give and serve. Furthermore, young people can be active in creating a positive norm for the whole congregation around giving and serving.

*The congregation's leadership articulates a commitment to giving and serving for all ages throughout the year.* Many observers point to the congregation's pastor or rabbi as setting the tone for a culture of generosity. Robert Leifert noted the influence of a New York synagogue's rabbi of 41 years, whose theme is "'Menschliness' before Godliness," referring to the Yiddish term mensch, an upright, caring, responsible person. "That is," Leifert explained, "before we can appeal to God, we must help our fellow man in order to stand before God." That theme, Leifert said, has created a clear expectation and emphasis on concern for the well-being of others throughout the congregation.

In addition to clear leadership from the pastor or rabbi, other leaders in the congregation also set a tone that creates an expectation of giving and serving. This may include those who work directly with children and youth, young people with leadership roles in the youth program or congregation, adult leaders in the congregation's board, and the informal leaders—those whom people recognize as leaders even when they do not have official positions.

Leaders have a variety of important roles in creating a culture that nurtures generosity. One may be to talk about it (and not just when a bill needs to be paid). Another is to be a model of generosity. A third may be to ask about it and encourage conversation about it. While these conversations may be uncomfortable or awkward at first, they make it clear that giving and serving are part of who the congregants are and what the congregation does.

*People of all ages are expected to give and serve.* In the congregations we interviewed where service and giving have become an integral and important part of young people's experience of that congregation, we noticed a clear sense that generosity was normative and expected. That expectation was particularly striking in the Jewish congregations where both *tzedakah* and *tikkun olam* are considered cornerstones of the congregation's culture. As Rabbi Neal Gold put it: "It sounds like a fantasy world, but it's really true. . . . [Young people] really believe fundamentally that doing *tikkun olam* is a fundamental aspect of what Jewish living is about."

Joseph Bailey ties an expectation to serve and give to his congregation's core theology:

> From a Lutheran perspective, we believe in . . . a priesthood of all believers. We don't have a priest; we are all priests—every single one of us. And we're all called to serve, we're all called to give, and we are all called to love. . . . And so from that perspective, it's not only important for youth to give and serve, it's a requirement. And if they're not doing it, then they have some questions to answer. More importantly, if the adults involved aren't leading and guiding the children in a way that makes giving and serving possible, then boy, do we have some questions to answer.

One of the times when congregations are most likely to require service involvement is during the confirmation or bar or bat mitzvah process. For example, the confirmation program at Catholic Community of the Sacred Heart in Jeffersonville, Indiana, has clear expectations of service to others. Confirmands are expected to participate in 14 projects—at least one in each of seven areas: family, peers/school, community, parish/larger church, special needs, elderly, and children. Several options are given in each category to match young people's talents and interests with projects.

*Symbols and reminders of giving and serving are prominent in the congregation.* Jules Gutin of the United Synagogue of Conservative Judaism suggested that one reason *tzedakah* giving is so prevalent among observant Jews is that there are constant reminders to give. For example, he said, if you go to a Jewish grocery store, a kosher butcher, Jewish bookstore, or other Jewish business, you'll find *tzedakah* boxes "lined up next to the cash register for all different kinds of organizations and institutions." When a *tzedakah* box or plate is passed at morning services, "some people put in a dollar every day, some put in 25 cents. But I rarely see people not putting something in."

Gutin recalled an incident when his teenage daughter stopped him on the way in to a weekday service because she realized she had forgotten her wallet. She asked, "Did you bring any money with you? Can I borrow a dollar from you so I can put it in the plate when we walk in?"

The specific symbols and reminders of the importance of generosity are inextricably tied to the congregation's specific faith tradition, culture, and identity. For many, the symbols can be an integral part of worship, such as, in Christian churches, the passing of an offering plate, a foot-washing ritual, or language about giving and serving integrated into the litanies and hymns. In other cases, they may include collection boxes for a charitable food shelf located prominently in the entryway to the congregation's worship space.

The reminders may include posters in the youth room or notices in the congregation's newsletter or worship bulletin. Mark Vincent described a subtle shift in how a congregation reports on its financial health in a congregation's bulletin. "Most churches . . . say every week what they need and what the gaps are according to a budgeted amount. Then once a year, they tell you how it was distributed. In contrast, he told of a congregation that, each week, reports on how much has been received and how it has been distributed. The shift, he suggested, focuses on the giver, the gift, and the need being addressed, rather than on the institutional needs.

*Giving and serving are integrated into all areas of congregational life.* If the goal is to create a culture where service and giving are normative, it's not enough to offer occasional service projects for youth while failing to reinforce those experiences and priorities in worship, religious education, and other areas of congregational life. Eileen Campbell-Reed, a Baptist, has found that "[service] has to be integrated into the life of the church. . . . If it's the priority of the whole church, as you do youth ministry, you seek to make that consistent in the ministry with youth. . . . If you are struggling with a church that doesn't prioritize a service ministry or hands-on involvement, it could be very hard to create that culture within the youth group."

*Young people inspire the congregation to engage in giving and serving.* A congregation's young people do not have to wait for adults to take the lead in creating a culture in which giving and serving are normative. Indeed, many leaders have found that engaging young people in service can, over time, transform the whole congregation. "Again and again, our congregation has said the youth are leading us in mission," reported Mary Kohlsdorff. "I think that the adults should inspire the youth by their actions," she continued. "But it's been kind of an opposite effect here."

LeRoy Wilke of the Lutheran Church–Missouri Synod, who was instrumental in starting that denomination's major Servant Projects emphasis, has seen young people's engagement in service as a catalyst for shifting congregational norms and culture. "The service action on the part of young people is causing . . . some adults to raise questions. 'Why is this going on? That's sure a different picture of teenagers than I've heard on the news or from other stories.' . . . And then after some of that inquisitive process, some adults . . . are beginning to ask, 'Can I participate in this, too?'" In time, he said, service projects initiated by the youth have as many or more adult participants as they do youth, with the generations working together.

While young people often are catalysts for a congregationwide commitment to service, there are fewer examples of young people being catalysts for strengthening norms of financial giving in congregations. But it does—and could—happen. Sylvia Ronsvalle of empty tomb, inc., told the story of a United Methodist congregation that had, because of financial constraints, gradually reduced its contributions to the denomination, international missions, and other causes. "They hadn't paid anything for years," she recalls.

As part of the process of shifting the church's stewardship efforts from a focus on institutional needs to a focus on mission, the pastor went to the youth group to explain how the congregation set its budget, including its apportionment to the denomination and other missional giving. That night the pastor's son, a youth group member, came home and reported that the youth group was furious that the congregation had eliminated its support for missions. Furthermore, one youth group member took a summer job and set aside 10 percent of his income for giving. But he stipulated that more of the money had to go outside the congregation.

As a result of this public activism, Ronsvalle said, "The men's group was so embarrassed that they made the world service apportionment their commitment." Instead of giving $20 or so at each monthly breakfast, they started to give between $150 and $200, she said.

A danger, of course, in the hope that young people will be catalysts for shifting congregational norms of giving and serving is that the congregation's involvement will stop with the young people and not transform the whole congregation. Mary Kohlsdorff said she worries: "It's important to me for the congregation to be just as involved in mission opportunities and not just let the youth do it." However, if young people are actively involved, and their actions are visible and valued in the congregation, their efforts can have a powerful influence on shaping a congregation where generosity is the norm and expectation.

# CHAPTER 7

# Cultivating the Practices of Generosity

The first four keys, discussed in chapter 6, set a context for giving and serving among young people. They address the congregation's commitments, priorities, norms, and traditions for giving and serving. They also emphasize the importance of young people having meaningful engagement in congregational life.

## PUTTING GENEROSITY INTO PRACTICE

The final four keys focus more specifically on the importance of offering young people, their families, and the intergenerational community meaningful, consistent, and concrete opportunities to practice both giving and serving. We intentionally use the word "practice" for two reasons:

First, we seek to connect with the renewed emphasis within the Christian tradition on "Christian practices," which emphasize a way of life, not a series of activities or programs. Craig Dykstra of the Lilly Endowment and Dorothy C. Bass of Valparaiso University write that Christian practices are "ordinary activities, the stuff of everyday life. Yet all of them, no matter how mundane, can be shaped in response to God's active presence. And all of them, woven together, suggest the patterns of a faithful Christian way of life."[1]

This recent emphasis on practice has parallels in the Jewish community. For example, Synagogue 2000, which focuses on the spiritual transformation of synagogues, focuses on essential practices of synagogue life: prayer, learning, good deeds, and healing.[2] Another example can be found in Rabbi Arthur Waskow's book *Down-to-Earth Judaism*, in which he seeks to rediscover wisdom and truth in traditions of Judaism that are relevant in everyday life, such as food, money, and sexuality. Or, as he puts it, "drawing on Jewish wisdom to shape our daily life-paths."[3]

The word "practice" also suggests a process and growth. It recognizes that giving and serving are actions we must first try and then repeat in order to learn. As Robert Wuthnow noted, "Practice is something you have to learn, you have to spend some time doing it—in fact, getting better at it one step at a time, learning from others, and so forth." He suggested that much more care is needed to help youth integrate giving into their self-understanding and their development as spiritual people.

## Key 5: Provide Opportunities for Youth to Practice Giving

Key 5 focuses specifically on providing young people with opportunities to give or share their money. We recognize the complexity of addressing financial giving with young people, as suggested by the entire chapter on the barriers to dealing with youth giving (chapter 3). We also acknowledge that different faith traditions and congregations have very different practices of giving.

In Jewish traditions, for example, members do not "give" to the congregation; rather, they pay dues. Jewish giving tends to focus more specifically on meeting needs and addressing injustices in the Jewish community and beyond. In contrast, most Christian churches focus primarily on giving to the congregation, with most gifts used to support the congregation's activities (including its missions or benevolence work). Thus, many specifics about how and where young people give can be unique to a specific faith tradition.

But the larger question that transcends these differences is the issue of cultivating ways that congregations provide opportunities for young people to "practice" giving. Dwight Burlingame of Indiana University's Center on Philanthropy noted that "we really lost traditions of having children participate in the giving process. . . . Giving part of [your allowance] back as a child as soon as you recognize what money is . . . is a very formative activity. If you only talk about it and not do it, it is not very formative."

This key provides a focal point for addressing the issues of being responsible with the financial resources that young people have at their disposal, whether the have a little or a lot. We have identified six elements in providing young people with the opportunities to practice financial giving.

*The congregation offers guidance and support in making faithful, responsible choices about money.* It is difficult, if not impossible, to help young people become consistent, generous givers without helping them develop a faithful, responsible understanding of and attitude toward money, materialism, and consumerism. "Until people can get out on the table what has influenced them about money or where they are realistically in their own lives about money," said Nathan Dungan of Lutheran Brotherhood, "I don't know that you have a shot at training and forming new habits of giving. . . . Until we get after the money within the formula of the whole, . . . to frame people to be good givers is virtually impossible."

A wide range of issues could be addressed in congregations (through sermons, youth programming, family education, intergenerational mentoring and conversations) that help young people connect their faith, beliefs, and values with their financial choices. These include:

- Exploration of the writings, traditions, and beliefs of their faith traditions about money, wealth, work, and materialism
- Assistance with learning responsible money management, including how to budget, earn, spend, save, and share on the basis of their values and priorities. Said Rabbi Dennis Eisner: "Any good budget should have a charity line. If you get an allowance of $50, one of your lines should be a charity line. Are we teaching that? I don't know. . . . We probably should be."
- Identification of stresses or struggles that young people and their families have in relation to money, poverty, or wealth
- Examination of the influence of media, advertising, peers, and family in priorities, choices, and stresses about money

In their book *At Ease: Discussing Money and Values in Small Groups,* John and Sylvia Ronsvalle suggest a three-stage process for small-group conversations about money that can provide a framework for meaningful discussions with young people:

- The first level focuses on understanding money from a faith perspective, including reflection on personal attitudes about money, giving, and spending, and the teachings of faith.
- The second level focuses on the practical issues of budgeting, including personal spending and giving patterns.

- The third level delves into deeper issues of trust, responsibility, and opportunity that are integral to growth in faith.[4]

These kinds of small-group discussions not only help young people think through issues of money and giving; they also offer an important support group for young people (and adults) as they struggle with being faithful with their money in a consumer-oriented world.

To be sure, the religious community is not united in its understanding of money and whether (or how much) it embraces or critiques a consumer culture. The range of opinion can be illustrated by divergent perspectives on money within the evangelical Christian community. On one end of the spectrum, according to historian Michael S. Hamilton of Seattle Pacific University, are those who embrace "the prosperity gospel" that insists, "God will reward a generous giver with yet greater financial return in this life." On the other end of the spectrum are the evangelicals who urge simplicity, renounce wealth, and "make themselves poor and then live with the poor." In the middle are those who advocate a style of financial management not unlike most financial counselors but with a strong emphasis on the obligation to tithe.[5]

A variety of resources, curricula, games, and other tools is available to help teach these kinds of issues to young people (see appendix A). However, perhaps even more important than teaching the content is providing the opportunities, relationships, role models, and sense of community that help young people deal with money at a more personal level.

At Heritage Baptist Church in Cartersville, Georgia, leaders conducted an in-depth financial study with high school youth in which they invited adults in the congregation to come talk with young people about stewardship and giving. According to Eileen Campbell-Reed, minister of Christian education, the leaders invited people who "have a good concept of whole-life stewardship ... an understanding that everything belongs to God. . . . We really integrated the idea of giving into [young people's] lives."

Addressing the broader financial choices that youth make not only lays the foundation for them to make giving an integral part of their economic life—it also offers them the permission, resources, language, and support to make wise, faithful economic choices in all areas of life. In the process, youth can begin to overcome the privatization and unhealthy silence about financial issues that can leave them vulnerable and isolated with the financial stresses that plague so many adults in this society.

*Young people are active decision makers in the giving process.*
One of the strengths of the Jewish community in terms of youth giving,
suggested Jeffrey Dekro of the Shefa Fund, is that young people "are involved in determining where they want the money to go—not just putting it
into a bag or tin that goes around and then the adults decide where the
money will go." He continued: "The most fundamental issue . . . is the
extent to which kids are being asked to talk about, think about, and make
real decisions about how they want to develop *tzedakah* programs."

Involving young people in the planning and decision-making for how
the money is used is important not only for increasing their commitment and
enthusiasm. It also provides opportunities for young people to become
thoughtful, responsible givers. When the process is taken seriously, youth
can learn how to determine where to contribute and how much to give to
various causes. They can learn ways to assess the integrity and quality of
organizations that seek funding. These skills lay an important foundation for
wise giving throughout their lives.

Dennis Eisner of Hebrew Union College–Jewish Institute of Religion
in Los Angeles is often invited to teach classes at UAHC Kutz Camp, the
national youth leadership development institute for the Reform movement.
One of the things he emphasizes in teaching young people about *tzedakah*
is how to give in a way that is responsible and honoring of others. He asks:
"What's the difference between walking down the street and having someone say, 'Can you spare some change?' and then digging through the bottom of your backpack and maybe find a nickel . . . [and] preparing yourself
as you go and . . . having a pocket full of change so that, as soon as somebody were to ask you for *tzedakah*, you don't have to dig?"

He also urges young people to be smart in their spontaneous giving.
"When you're walking down the street of New York City and someone
asks you for some change, don't reach into your backpack and pull out your
wallet with all your money. That's not smart. But be prepared and have the
right kind of *tzedakah* money to give to somebody."

*Young people are encouraged and guided to plan their giving.* An
important way to emphasize an expectation of giving is to encourage young
people to plan their giving through pledging or percentage giving (such as a
tithe). This approach not only is likely to generate higher levels of giving, but
it also challenges young people and recognizes them as contributors and
resources for the congregation, not just recipients of services.

An emphasis on planning for giving adds consistency. It's important to note that not all traditions emphasize planning or pledging. In some traditions, the majority of giving is spontaneous in response to a need, appeal, or individual. Yet even in these situations, young people are much less likely to be able to give spontaneously if they do not manage their money and plan to give a portion of it away.

In addition, congregations have important opportunities not only to help young people plan their giving to their congregation (which tends to be the emphasis in most Christian congregations), but also to other worthy causes and organizations. Such an approach recognizes the reality that people who give tend to give to many organizations. It also underscores the congregation's role in helping young people be responsible with all of their financial resources, not just those contributed to the congregation.

*Emphasis is placed on the habit of giving, not the amount given.* The widespread focus on meeting institutional needs or raising a particular amount of money typically shifts attention from young people (who tend not to give much money) to older adults, who are more likely to give enough to pay the bills or meet financial goals. In the process, young people are not nurtured to begin to develop the lifetime practice of giving.

The focus on the habit of giving is clearly consistent with both Jewish and Christian teaching. Furthermore, it helps to address three concerns that people raise when asked to consider asking young people to give.

First, it responds to the reality that too many young people live in poverty. But instead of simply saying, "We shouldn't ask them because they don't have much," it's important to view and teach giving as an opportunity and act of faith for all young people, including those who are poor. Dwight Burlingame of Indiana University's Center on Philanthropy observed: "The art of giving is a gentle act of love. To suggest that I should be deprived of the joy that I can receive from giving because I don't have as much as someone else is just downright foolish."

Second, it recognizes that developing the habit of giving is a long-term process. For those young people who have been practicing giving since they were young children, the challenge may be substantially different that facing a young person who is being asked to give for the first time.

Finally, this focus begins to address the concern raised by those who worry that asking young people to give will scare them off—particularly if the congregation is reaching out to unaffiliated youth. Thom Schultz suggests that part of the solution is also to choose the right moment and manner to address the issue of giving with youth. "We can find ways that we can layer our ministry so that we don't have to worry about . . . [new] kids being turned off because we are asking for money," he said. "But as kids move in faith maturity, . . . [giving] can be talked about . . . [as] a normal part of their faith and church life."

*Young people can see tangible results from their giving.* An important way to reinforce giving in ways that encourage young people to keep giving is for them to see tangible results. Too often, though, giving in congregations isn't tangible. As a young woman from a Baptist church said: "If you just give money in the offering plate, it's going to a variety of different things. And I know those are important. But I don't know exactly what those are."

Directing giving toward tangible things has been a critical part of the giving efforts at Ankeny (Iowa) Presbyterian Church. One year, the young people bought school supplies for children who didn't have them. Another year, the children in vacation Bible school contributed money to buy an animal for a farmer in the developing world. "We knew if we got a certain amount of money we could either buy a chicken or goat or a cow for a family," recalled youth director Mary Kohlsdorff. "Each day, at the end of the day, [the young people] announced how much money we had made that day and where we were in terms of our goal. . . . The kids were so excited . . .they brought in more and more money each day." In the end, they raised enough to buy a cow. The children learned, Kohlsdorff found, that each small contribution they brought each day added up.[6]

*Young people have opportunities to talk about and reflect on their financial giving.* An important way to provide guidance and support is to offer opportunities for young people to talk about money and financial giving. Indeed, according to Thom Schultz, "[Growth] won't happen without debriefing and talking about it." He noted that "once we run through that campaign about giving more, we really don't talk much about or process much about what it means in our lives on an ongoing basis and how it affects us and others."

Note that these conversations focus on self-reflection on lifestyle, faith, and choices about money, not primarily on institutional needs. James P. Wind suggested that "there needs to be a different kind of talk about money in congregations that is uncoupled from the needs of the budget."

Robert Wood Lynn added: "Too much of the contemporary literature deals with the question of how much, and not nearly enough attention is given to the consequences of our giving upon other people. Do we make them dependent upon us? Do we insist that they express gratitude? Are these wise gifts? Money is often very destructive when it comes to people in the form of a gift, and we do almost nothing in most mainline churches to help people reflect on their giving."

Such conversations are not easy to lead. To spark a group discussion about money, the youth leaders at Heritage Baptist Church in Cartersville, Georgia, had youth group members imagine that they had graduated from college and had a job. "We gave them the salary, and we gave them a list of the things they had to buy," recalled Eileen Campbell-Reed. Though it was a fairly simple exercise in budgeting, "it was overwhelming to them," she recalled. "It was really interesting how it stressed them out completely to even talk about their financial situation."

Within the Jewish community, it is not unusual for people to share openly information about their money in ways that encourage them to be responsible with how they spend and share their resources. Dennis Eisner described how he and other rabbinical students formed a *tzedakah* collective in which they pooled their contributions to give more responsibly "to the right people and the right places." The first year, the participants contributed and disbursed $4,000. Now, several years later and spread out throughout the country at different assignments, the former students have continued pooling their contributions. The practice has been a useful teaching tool in working with youth.

Another example can be found in the traditions of the Mennonites and Quakers. Sharon Daloz Parks tells of a Mennonite congregation in the Midwest that requires all members to be part of a small group. At least once each year, each group talks together about household economics—the money each group member earned, spent, saved, and shared. These exchanges, Parks suggests, help people make more faithful choices. "As lone individuals, it is very difficult to change our economic patterns."[7] While these examples focus on adults, they have potential for young people who could benefit from the same kind of supportive guidance.

## KEY 6: OFFER OPPORTUNITIES FOR YOUTH TO PRACTICE SERVING

Service projects, social-action projects, mission trips, work camps, and other service experiences are the "training ground" for a lifetime of serving others. Robert Wuthnow writes:

[V]olunteering is the route by which young people move from a primordial understanding of caring—rooted in family ties—to a more specialized understanding that will serve them better as they assume responsibilities in complex social institutions. Volunteering is thus an important link between having good intentions and being able to put them into practice. . . . By doing community service, young people make the critical transition from familial caring to a more mature understanding of kindness.[8]

Because of the growing emphasis on youth service in recent decades (see chapter 4), much attention has been focused on how to make service or volunteering most effective. A growing body of research and experience suggests that "service-learning" offers the most effective models and approaches to engaging youth in service. While the field continues to debate how exactly to define the term service-learning,[9] it essentially suggests two key elements:

- *Service*: Young people engage in activities that meet the needs of others and the community.
- *Learning*: The experiences of serving others is used as an opportunity for self-reflection and learning.

The potential benefits of service-learning are many. But researchers and practitioners have found that not all service-learning experiences are equal. For example, in analyzing the results of a Search Institute study of school-based service-learning among middle school students, researcher Peter C. Scales writes: "The students who were involved in high-quality, well-run service-learning programs fared better than their peers who were in lesser-quality programs or did no service-learning. The best service-learning experiences included plenty of service and a substantial amount of time for students to reflect through writing and discussions with peers, teachers, parents, community members, and others."[10]

Because of the power of a service-learning approach, we have focused the dimensions of this key around a basic, four-part service-learning process, as summarized in figure 11 (on the following page).[11]

# Figure 11

## The PARR Process for Service-Learning

The PARR process for service-learning, highlighted here, outlines the four
key phases in organizing a service-learning project or program.
Effective efforts put energy into all four areas.

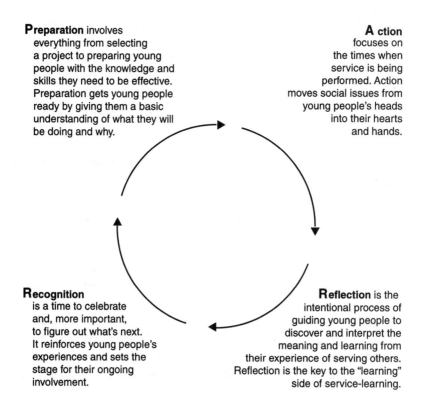

**P**reparation involves
everything from selecting
a project to preparing young
people with the knowledge and
skills they need to be effective.
Preparation gets young people
ready by giving them a basic
understanding of what they will
be doing and why.

**A**ction
focuses on
the times when
service is being
performed. Action
moves social issues from
young people's heads
into their hearts
and hands.

**R**ecognition
is a time to celebrate
and, more important,
to figure out what's next.
It reinforces young people's
experiences and sets the
stage for their ongoing
involvement.

**R**eflection is the
intentional process of
guiding young people to
discover and interpret the
meaning and learning from
their experience of serving others.
Reflection is the key to the "learning"
side of service-learning.

Adapted with permission from Eugene C. Roehlkepartain, Tom Bright, and
Beth Margolis-Rupp, *An Asset Builder's Guide to Service-Learning*
(Minneapolis: Search Institute, 2000), 4.

*Young people take an active leadership role in planning and leading service activities.* Young people's active leadership in service-learning efforts is important to the project's success and to the youth's own growth. Arva Rice of Public Allies in New York City reported: "Some of the most effective service I've seen . . . involves the young people and asks them to identify what they think are the primary issues."

Rich Junghans of St. Michael's Catholic Church in Stillwater, Minnesota, agreed. It's critical, he said, to "put the kids in leadership roles and really let them take ownership of the projects as much as possible . . . not just coming in the day that the work's going to be done." In his experience, he added, "The kids really like to . . . be involved in the planning and the promotion and getting kids lined up to be part of the project. When they feel [that] they have an investment in [a project], they really want to see it be completed and done well."

At Temple Israel in Minneapolis, a key way of involving young people is encouraging them constantly to look for places where they could be involved in the community, individually or as a group. The result, said Heidi Tarshish, is that youth are actively involved in many ways. Sometimes they discover opportunities for the whole group to engage in social action together. At other times, teenagers identify things that they can do on their own—things "that are very different [from] what we have offered."

The point, said Tarshish, is to help all young people discover what they have to contribute. "We have to look at everybody individually," she said. "Everybody has something to offer."

*Service experiences are thoughtfully planned to address real community needs as well as the growth and development of young people.* Preparation focuses on the key tasks in getting ready for a service-learning project. Through this stage, young people learn how to assess opportunities and needs, design a project in response to those needs, begin learning the information they need to be effective as learners and contributors, and develop the skills they will need. Of course, young people play central roles throughout the preparation process.

Many congregations that participate in youth work camps provide extensive preparation. Mary, Mother of the Church, a Roman Catholic congregation in Burnsville, Minnesota, sponsors an annual spring-break work trip to Mexico. To prepare for the trip, young people must perform service in the local community and attend five three-hour training and team-building meetings, in which young people learn about the culture and people of

Guaymas, Mexico. These meetings also clarify expectations for both the youth and adults who will participate in the trip.[12]

*Young people have ongoing opportunities to serve others.* The action phase varies considerably, depending on the type of project, location, the age and size of the group involved, and many other factors. In general, however, a number of tasks help make serving others a positive, life-enriching experience for young people. These include:

- Establishing clear assignments, expectations, and schedules
- Keeping a focus on learning and development goals
- Promoting interpersonal and cultural sharing
- Providing supervision and ensuring safety
- Meeting ongoing training needs
- Keeping parents, other youth, and other members of the congregation connected
- Documenting experiences and preparing for reflection

At least three important issues must be addressed in the action phase. First is an emphasis on *ongoing* opportunities to serve others. The research on service-learning consistently shows that the more often young people are involved in service, the greater the impact. Furthermore, ongoing involvement (whether it's in a single project or in a series of smaller projects over time) reinforces and builds on the skills and commitment to serving others. Lyn Baird writes: "Service-learning achieves its full value only if it leads to an enduring life-style of continued personal development and concern for others. A one-shot inoculation will not provide lasting immunization against the social malady of self-interest. The impulse to serve needs to be nurtured over time."[13]

The challenge is that too many congregations place all their emphasis on a single project or trip, neglecting the need for ongoing involvement in service and learning throughout the year. Such a single-minded focus misses a rich opportunity for growth, as illustrated by this example:

Dean Feldmeyer, a United Methodist pastor, tells about a youth group in a former congregation where young people visited the nursing home monthly to lead recreation and make friends. As the weeks passed, young people began building strong relationships with "someone completely out of their frame of experience."

They would send cards and call on the phone between visits. If one of the "regulars" was missing from a recreation time, the youth would go searching through the nursing home to find the person. . . . Not only did the youth hear the stories and perspectives of another generation, they also struggled with issues of death and dying when their friends in the home passed away.[14]

In addition to providing a single project that is sustained across time, some congregations nurture ongoing involvement by providing a variety of opportunities for young people to serve, ranging from simple, short-term activities through in-depth experiences. Such an approach not only appeals to young people's individual needs and preferences, but it also provides access points for young people based on their current commitment to and experiences of serving others.

Fellowship Evangelical Free Church in Knoxville, Tennessee, includes a wide variety of service opportunities, many of them quick and easy, according to Alan Ramsey, junior high pastor. Like many other youth groups, he said, "we'll go in and work with an inner-city church or an inner-city organization and do . . . home repair work, paint, scrape and yard work and things like that." In addition, the youth group does a variety of other things they call "random acts of loving-kindness." "We'll just take the kids and go to a gas station and pump people's gas and wash their windows, [for] no other reason, but just to love people and to serve them," he said.

A second issue is how to ensure that the projects are appropriate for the youth who are serving. This question can be a factor for both the whole group as well as with individuals.

Heidi Tarshish of Temple Israel remembers one student who became very negative about the various jobs in a service project—particularly the task of cleaning bathrooms. She approached him and explained that "some *mitzvahs* are easier to do than others and . . . that when we do this community service work it's not always for us—we are doing for others." But she didn't stop there. "We've got to find something that you are really going to feel good about when you go," she insisted. After some talking, she learned that the young man loved photography, so he became the official photographer for various events, fund-raisers, and service projects. "It has been phenomenal," Tarshish concludes. "This student really came around and really found things that he could contribute and do, and benefit from, and get positive recognition."

A different challenge is present when Our Savior's Lutheran Church in Box Elder, Montana, seeks to engage young people in service, said Pastor Joseph Bailey. The challenge is overcoming the stereotypes people have regarding low-income Native American youth—and the embarrassment that some of these young people feel about their lives. Too often, Bailey said, the young people can get into situations (such as a summer camp) where they feel embarrassed about their lack of financial resources. "They don't want to go because they are not going to have the clothes and the fancy sleeping bag," he explained.

One strategy Bailey uses is to select projects where the young people feel more comfortable. Recently, for example, the junior high group hosted a party for the nearby Bear Paw Youth Guidance Home. "These are all kids that have been in trouble," Bailey explained, "and those kids were 'safe' for our kids. Our kids understood that these kids were marginalized in a way." Each group member bought gifts for the children, had a picnic with them, then took them out for ice cream. "Boy, was it fun for our kids!" Bailey recalls.

A third issue to address in the action phase is the value of tapping into existing opportunities to serve rather than always creating new opportunities. These resources may include other congregations, local agencies, ecumenical or interfaith coalitions, denominational programs, and independent organizations that sponsor service projects. Connecting with these organizations not only can reduce the logistical workload, but it can also expose young people to a much wider array of issues and people than might be possible if the congregation planned all its own independent service projects.

*Young people have opportunities to reflect on their service involvement.* We have emphasized at several points the importance of intentional reflection as part of effective service-learning (see, for example, chapter 5). Perhaps the best way to re-emphasize the importance of reflection is to quote service-learning pioneers Dan Conrad and Diane Hedin: "To say that experience is a good teacher . . . does not imply that it's easily or automatically so. If it were, we'd all be a lot wiser than we are. It's true that we can learn from experience. We may also learn nothing. Or we may, like Mark Twain's cat who learned from sitting on a hot stove lid never to sit again, learn the wrong lesson."[15]

Reflection can take many forms and take place both during the service experience and afterward. While there are many approaches to reflection,[16] a common framework builds on the educational theory of David Kolb, who developed the experiential learning cycle.[17] Service-learning expert Kate McPherson simplifies the language of Kolb's cycle and suggests three key questions to guide reflection:[18]

- Concrete experience: Participating in a direct, immediate experience (e.g., a service project)
- Reflective observation (What?): Examining the experience in light of beliefs, values, and previous knowledge
- Abstract conceptualization (So what?): Creating ideas, concepts, and new learning that organize the experience and its meaning
- Active experimentation (Now what?): Testing or applying the learning or concepts in new situations

In addition to allowing young people to move from concrete experiences to more abstract ideas and learning, the experiential learning cycle invites people with different learning styles to participate fully. As was first suggested in *Beyond Leaf Raking*, this reflection process can also be enriched and directly linked to growth in faith by connecting it to Thomas Groome's "shared praxis" approach to religious education.[19] Below, we highlight the parallels:

| ELEMENTS OF SERVICE-LEARNING CYCLE | GROOME'S 'MOVEMENTS' OF SHARED PRAXIS |
|---|---|
| What? | 1. Looking at life |
| So what? | 2. Reflecting on life |
| | 3. Knowing our faith |
| | 4. Making the faith our own |
| Now what? | 5. Living our faith[20] |

While reflection is important, it is not essential that it follow a specific format or be rigid or formal. It can be encouraged throughout the service-learning process, not just as a final debriefing. Indeed, the specifics of reflection can vary widely, depending on the situation and group. Sometimes it is best when it is a spontaneous response to a "teachable moment" that comes in the midst of serving.

Cherie Smith of Kirkwood (Missouri) Baptist Church recounted an incident from a work trip her church's youth group took to an inner-city church in Louisville. Planned reflection became the key to deeper understanding. "I picked [the church] on purpose because they have a woman pastor who's white in this inner-city church. When they had enough money for a second staff member, they hired a minister to the homeless instead of youth or music minister or whatever."

Smith described how the group worked hard, hosting a vacation Bible school for neighborhood children, cleaning out a basement, weeding a garden. "We did really hard work," Smith recalled. "It was tough for us, and [some group members] whined some. They thought it was going to be fun. I kept trying to tell them, 'You guys, [service] is not always fun.'"

On the final evening of the trip, the group sat together to talk about what they would say when they reported their experiences back home through leading a worship service. "That was when we could tell that this trip had really affected them," Smith recalled. The Scriptures young people picked and the hymns they selected, and the stories they prepared to tell all showed how the experience had deepened a sense of commitment to serving others.

*Young people's acts of service are recognized, affirmed, and celebrated by the whole congregation.* For lasting change and growth to occur, the primary motivation needs to be intrinsic to the service that's being performed. Adding incentives or recognition for young people's service risks shifting focus away from the intrinsic value of service to an emphasis on extrinsic rewards. At the same time, when the service is done well, rewards, recognition, and reinforcement can help to overcome inertia, help people get started, and help maintain momentum, particularly for large, long-term goals.

The process of recognition not only celebrates what has been done; it also increases the congregation's engagement with and commitment to service. It helps to solidify young people's commitment both to service and to the issues behind their efforts. An emphasis on recognition can be the vehicle for young people to become catalysts for broader congregational involvement in service. Mary Kohlsdorff described how the young people in her church share their experiences after returning from a mission trip. "You can't help but be moved when you hear these kids, who are 15 to 18, talking about how God has changed their life. . . . Their openness and willingness to share has really affected our congregation."

## KEY 7: SUPPORT FAMILIES

Families play a critical role in young people's commitments to giving and serving. As noted in chapter 5, many factors that lay the foundation for a lifestyle of generosity have their roots in the family. Diana Mendley Rauner writes:

> Caring habits and skills are primarily passed along from parents to children, from generation to generation, as parents consciously and unconsciously convey messages about the child's responsibilities and roles in her environment through explicit instruction, expectations, modeling and reinforcement. Such values are reinforced in the child's contact with other adults in her family and in the important institutions of her culture.[21]

Such a perspective is clearly supported by many of the people we interviewed. For example, Nathan Dungan, who leads Lutheran Brotherhood's efforts to address financial stewardship with children, youth, and families, said he believes that "money lessons are either won or lost in the home." Indeed, a 1998 Harris Poll found that parents are the main source of advice for teenagers about managing money, with 43 percent of young people identifying their mother as having taught them the most about managing money, and 29 percent identifying their father.[22]

Similarly, strong connections exist between young people's own engagement and service and their parents' involvement. Search Institute research shows, for example, that two-thirds (66 percent) of young people who strongly agree that their parents "spend a lot of time helping other people" also report doing at least one hour of volunteer work "in an average week." In contrast, among young people who strongly disagree that their parents spend a lot of time helping others, only 32 percent are engaged in any volunteer work.[23]

In contrast, an effort on the part of parents can be a powerful force in young people's lives. Dennis Eisner described how he and his wife began to create an expectation of generosity with their newborn: "When our son was born, the first thing we put in his room was a *tzedakah* box. He's 11 weeks old—he has no idea. But he will. He will know that it exists and that it's his and that it's in his room and it's his job, when he gets birthday money, not only to put it away for himself, but to put part of it in the *tzedakah* box."

Despite the opportunity to tap the tremendous influence of families, many congregations do little to support and equip parents to be effective in articulating, acting, and passing on the traditions of giving and serving to their children. Such support is essential. Families cannot do the job alone; too many other social forces can interfere with these commitments. Yet many parents did not experience these commitments in their own families of origin. Though they may wish to engage in giving and serving with their children, they may not be clear how to do it.

In cases where families already have strong family traditions and practices of giving and serving, congregations may be able to assume a role of prompting and reinforcing the lessons, values, and practices that are already being inculcated in the home. But parents who have not developed those practices need basic support, direction, opportunities, and guidance to help them become active partners in nurturing generosity in their children.

A growing number of resources focus on the variety of ways congregations can work in partnership with families.[24] Many of the themes in these general approaches to family ministry or family services can be infused with an emphasis on giving and serving. Four approaches can help equip families to be more effective in cultivating the practices of generosity their offspring.

*The congregation views parents as key partners in nurturing generosity in young people.* Most observers agree that families are the foundation of society and the center for faith nurture. For example, John Roberto writes (from a Catholic perspective):

> We believe that family life is sacred and that family activities are holy, that God's love is revealed and communicated in new ways each and every day through Christian families. We believe that the family is the *domestic church* or the *church of the home* and that the family shares in one and the same mission that Christ gives to the whole church. . . . We believe that effective ministry with families involves building a partnership between the congregation and the home, which focuses on the unique responsibilities that each [have] in promoting faith growth. . . . There is no more important task for congregations today than to promote the faith growth of families.[25]

However, a difficult challenge in partnering with families is that such a perspective is rarely implemented. Too many parents may have abdicated their faith-nurturing role to the congregation. And many congregations subtly convey the message that families should support congregations, not the other way around. Writing to Christian churches, Merton P. Strommen and Richard A. Hardel argue that "the current paradigm has subtly conveyed the impression that faith is nurtured only in the church building. . . . Over the years, the message has been, 'Let the professionals do the teaching. They know best.' So, parents send their children to church for Sunday school or other religious instruction, handing the responsibility of faith education to the teachers."[26]

An important priority for recognizing families as partners in nurturing giving and serving is to help families discover their mission. "Each family needs to discern and develop its own unique mission," write Richard P. Olson and Joe H. Leonard Jr. "This stands at the heart of a family ministry strategy."[27]

Perhaps the most comprehensive and provocative vision of the role of families in nurturing generosity can be found in Kathleen and James McGinnis's landmark book, *Parenting for Peace and Justice*. Writing from the perspective of Catholic activist parents, the McGinnises write that "our commitment to parenting can be precisely one of the basic ways in which we can answer the call to justice and peace. Rather than experiencing frustration at how little time is 'left over' for social concerns, we discover that parenting abounds with ways to integrate social concerns into daily life."[28] The McGinnises examine how a faith commitment to justice and peace can shape many areas of family life—from money to diet to relationships to social action. They write: "We want our children to experience social action as a regular part of family life. . . . If social action is experienced by children as a 'special extra,' tacked on if there is time, then it may well remain that way for them as adults."[29]

While congregations are not the focus of their work, the book offers a far-reaching challenge for thinking about how family life can nurture deep values and priorities. The question for congregations might be, What kind of community do we need to be to unleash and support many families to embody the deep commitments to generosity, compassion, and justice similar to those described by the McGinnises?

*The congregation integrates a family perspective into giving and serving activities.* John Roberto writes: "Creating a partnership with families does not necessitate designing new programming. It is extremely important to begin with your current ministries and programs and determine how well they address the needs of families. Making adjustments in your current programming is the first step toward creating a partnership with families."[30]

Ben Freudenberg suggests that a typical stewardship campaign in Christian churches can be reframed around families. "Instead of simply asking for money, we can help families learn how to become financially secure," he writes. "We can offer programs that help each family member develop positive Christian financial patterns in his or her life—including God's expectation for giving. A home-centered stewardship drive would give families opportunities to learn ways to manage their time, talents, and assets."[31]

*The congregation provides parents with support, education, and resources to inspire and equip them to encourage giving and serving in the home.* One of the first areas in which congregations often place energy is in discovering ways to support, educate, and equip parents to address giving and serving in the home. Such support and education is a vital link to correcting the imbalance between congregation and family. In *The Family-Friendly Church*, Ben Freudenburg suggests:

> Parents are so used to the church planning their children's faith-development journeys that they don't feel they have permission or the know-how to choose what's best for their kids. We need to empower and equip parents to make good choices for their family's faith development. That means we'll need to teach them about their role, encourage them to embrace it, give them training and resources to do it at home, and then pattern our church's programming and structure to support them in their role.[32]

Congregations can play important roles in educating parents about their potential for shaping their children's lives and in equipping parents with skills and tools that can help them nurture generosity in young people. This may include:

- Encouraging parents to reflect on their influence as role models for their children (in ways that either support or inhibit generosity)
- Supporting and guiding parents as they struggle with the stresses of time, money, vocation, and priorities that affect their ability to deal with these issues with their children
- Challenging parents to be more open in discussing money and giving with their children—and giving them opportunities to sort through their own anxieties and discomfort about money

- Providing parents with tools and resources to use at home to address issues of giving and serving throughout childhood and adolescence

Parent education is an important theme for youth work at Temple Israel in Minneapolis. Heidi Tarshish explained that the temple regularly sends parents information about the activities the young people are doing as well as material to help educate the parents on the issues. At each grade level, the temple has a family education component that includes parents. "This program really, really depends on parental involvement," Tarshish said. "Parents come with us on our field trips. Parents supervise sites, and siblings oftentimes come along. So it's a family event [with] parents . . . modeling the service piece with their kids."

When it comes to issues of giving and finances, Nathan Dungan of Lutheran Brotherhood has found that a powerful strategy is to bring parents and youth together to talk "so that they can hear what other kids are saying and what other parents are saying." He found that these kinds of interactions help both the young people and their parents see the other's perspective and open up dialogue as never before. In addition, the strategy provides a sense of support among families and "validates that they are not alone."[33]

*The congregation offers opportunities for families to serve together.* Providing families the chance to serve others together is a powerful strategy not only for nurturing generosity, but also for helping young people grow in faith. A Search Institute study of Protestant congregations found that involvement in family service projects during childhood and adolescence has a powerful impact on young people's growth in faith. Yet only about one-third of Protestant youth report much involvement in family service projects.[34] Nonetheless, there appears to be growing interest in family service. Thom Shultz said that his organization receives more and more requests for family-oriented work camps.

Family-oriented service projects offer opportunities for families to spend time together doing meaningful work, along with a context for talking about the family's values, priorities, beliefs, and worldview. "Family volunteering helps develop . . . stronger bonds by allowing family members to see each other in new roles and gain new appreciation for each other," says Virginia T. Austin of the Points of Light Foundation. "Adults are no longer automatic leaders. Volunteering as a family gives young people the opportunity to lead and direct."[35]

One of the potential challenges in engaging families in serving others is the stress already placed on families in a fast-paced world. Does this focus only add to the demands? While he agrees that many families may not naturally gravitate to serving others, Leif Kehrwald, consultant to St. Mary's Press, suggests that serving others can have a healing, renewing effect on families. "Faced with so many problems of their own," he writes, "many families are not motivated to serve others. Yet often, acts of selfless mercy can transform woes into healing as well as bring help to those in greater need."[36]

Designing service-learning experiences with families in mind is a high priority for St. John of the Cross Catholic Church in Middlebury, Connecticut, said Tom Bright, the parish's justice coordinator. The parish found that families really wanted to be involved, but they didn't know how and were uncomfortable engaging in service by themselves without guidance.

The parish identified a variety of service opportunities and hosted a service fair at which families heard about possibilities for involvement. Families were asked to commit to one of the options. Later someone from the parish followed up. The parish's goal was to move families toward greater involvement and commitment.

One year, families were invited to help refresh the facilities of a homeless shelter in a nearby community. For a day, families painted and cleaned. In the process, they were exposed to the need, became comfortable with being there, and had the satisfaction of seeing immediate results.

The next year, the congregation organized people who had experience serving in the shelter who were willing to be mentors for other interested families. The mentors visited with the families to prepare them for their experience, then served alongside them on their first evening in the shelter. Afterward, they reflected together about the experience. Before long, many of the families were comfortable and committed to serving in the shelter on a monthly basis.

## KEY 8: CONNECT GENERATIONS

We live in a time when—at least according to conventional wisdom—most people believe that they do not have responsibility for other generations. This society has given to parents and professionals (teachers, youth workers, day-care providers) almost total responsibility for raising the young. (Similarly, we assume that the professionals who staff nursing homes and other assisted-living situations are solely responsible for people at the other end of the age spectrum.) This assumption (which is much less true in minority communities) has undermined a sense of intergenerational community and created, to a large measure, an age-segregated society in which many people interact primarily, if not exclusively, with people of their own age. This situation undermines our ability as a society—and as communities of faith—to transmit the values and priorities that we hold dear from one generation to the next.

The final key to nurturing youth giving and serving is to make sure they see these practices being lived out by many members of the congregation, reinforcing the lessons learned at home and in other settings. Not only do young people need giving and serving role models (or "heroes"), they need to be in ongoing relationships with people of all ages so that they are exposed to the values and priorities of faith—including the priorities and practices of generosity.

This eighth key has received much less attention in the congregations we contacted and in the literature on giving and serving. Most congregations—particularly those that are predominantly white—have assumed that the congregation's engagement with youth and giving comes primarily through youth programs and families. However, given the importance of shaping a culture of generosity, it seems clear that an untapped resource within congregations is an array of intergenerational relationships. Through these connections, all members of the congregation can recognize their opportunity and responsibility for being mentors (formal or informal) for young people.

Evidence to support the power of intergenerational relationships can be found in Search Institute's ongoing research on youth in communities. In this comprehensive survey, we ask young people to report on the number of adults they have known for two or three years who "spend a lot of time helping other people" (the kinds of relationships that are possible in many congregations). Among the young people who reported none (about 18 percent of all the youth surveyed), only 27 percent also reported spending at least an hour in an average week doing volunteer work. On the other hand, among those who said that they were connected to five or more adults who spent a lot of time helping others, 65 percent of young people reported volunteering an hour or more.[37]

We suggest that there are at least three important dimensions to building bridges between youth and adults in connection with nurturing generosity: (1) adults recognizing their responsibility, (2) adults serving as role models, and (3) adults and youth engaging in giving and serving together.

*All adults in the congregation understand their responsibility to nurture, guide, and care for young people.* This first dimension focuses on overcoming the widespread cultural assumption that parents and professionals are solely responsible for nurturing generosity in young people. If congregations are to create a culture of generosity, it is essential to recognize that every member of the congregation has a role to play and a responsibility to nurture, guide, and care for young people.

It should be noted that such an assumption is tied primarily to the dominant "Anglo" culture of U.S. society (a culture that has shaped most of the literature on youth work in U.S. congregations). In contrast, Don Ng of First Chinese Baptist Church in San Francisco clearly sees the power of intergenerational responsibility within the culture of his congregation, which he attributes in large measure to the congregation's roots in Asian culture. "Our adults have served in the past to help young [people] to grow in their faith," he explains. "When the young people grow up and become responsible young adults, they feel an obligation to give back to the community what they have already received."

The goal in cultivating a widespread sense of responsibility for the young is not simply to get more adults to volunteer in youth programs. The goal is for young people to be surrounded by adults and peers who express care, offer guidance, talk with youth, and make it a habit to be supportive and nurturing.

In some congregations, the sense of connections across generations grows more easily because of history, cultural identity, or size. (It tends to be more common in smaller congregations that have not adopted a more formal, staff-oriented structure for congregational life.) That is the case at Beth Jacob Congregation in Mendota Heights, Minnesota, according to Wendy Schwartz, education and program director. "The fact that we have a wide spread of generations [makes it essential] that people do need to adopt each other, so to speak, and become connected." Such connections become evident, she said, when they see "junior high kids inviting . . . our esteemed seniors to their bar and bat mitzvahs just because they feel like they are sort of family."

Schwartz added: "I can't say that it's because of a program we ran, as much as I believe it's because of the nature of the *shul* [congregation] and the values of the *shul*." In addition, she noted, "These seniors don't necessarily have a family, and our young families don't necessarily have a grandparent that goes here. So they sort of naturally connect."

While some adult-to-youth connections can form more naturally or easily, there is often a need to educate adults about young people and how to relate to them in ways that are supportive and empowering. Cherie Smith of Kirkwood (Missouri) Baptist Church tells about her congregation's soup kitchen, where adults do not always welcome the young people as coworkers. "They don't say, 'Oh, we're glad you're here,'" Smith explained. "They don't say anything unless the kid makes a mistake. [Then they say], 'Hey, don't use that pan. Use this pan.' Or, 'You don't have your gloves on.'" She continued: "They don't mean to be critical. They think they are being helpful. That really tends to discourage the kids from taking initiative."

Smith is working to create a different response: "If [the young people] show up, and the team says: 'Oh, we're so glad you're here; we could really use your help—Jason, could you take this knife and go chop up these carrots?'" then they're valued and they're given responsibility and they're nurtured along. It really has to do with adults working shoulder to shoulder, helping them see that they're able."

*Young people have role models for giving and serving in the congregation.* Adults in the congregation must recognize that their values and life choices influence younger generations. For example, it's easy to frown on youthful materialism. But adults must always remember that young people's materialism mirrors what they see permeating adults' lives as well—the status placed on cars, where people live, the facilities in which people worship, and the ways people contribute their time and money. As Sylvia Ronsvalle asks, "If, in fact, adults are not giving, why would we expect children to be virtuous?"

Studies of philanthropy in African-American churches (which have tended to maintain more of an intergenerational focus) reinforce the importance of intergenerational models. For example, researchers from the Indiana University Center on Philanthropy found the following in a study of African-American philanthropy in the Midwest:

> The greatest means of inculcating traditions of giving and serving in the African-American church comes from the congregation itself. Members of the congregation who contribute time and money to the church serve as role models whom the young people observe, bolstering the example set by their parents. . . . [M]ost of the respondents spoke of their parents' financial support for the church even during difficult times, of their eagerness to volunteer at church functions, and of their willingness to support the

congregation's efforts to assist those in need. Many see themselves as continuing their parents' church-based legacy.[38]

Congregations can find many ways to nurture role models of generosity in the congregation. A fairly widespread approach is to invite adults
(usually older adults) to visit with the youth group, telling their own story and
inviting dialogue. Sylvia Ronsvalle suggests that a powerful strategy for
helping young people with issues of giving is "to tell the stories of giving and
make sure that the kids hear them through matching older and younger
people." She tells of visiting many congregations and finding only one or
two people who "would start talking to us about their own experience. . . .
If people are embarrassed to stand up in front of the whole congregation,
they may not be embarrassed to tell the children why they give . . . or where
they learned to give."

Adults cannot be role models or mentors in giving and serving if those
practices are not part of their own lives. Congregationwide planning, engagement, education, and reflection become important foundational strategies in creating a culture of generosity.

*The congregation provides opportunities for all generations to
give and serve together.* Though it's clearly an overstatement, many congregations have split giving and serving by generation: The adults give; the
youth serve. What happens when all generations do both together? Such "in
practice" connections can become opportunities for transmitting values and
habits. They also nurture the relationships that help to integrate youth into
congregational life and strengthen connections to the congregation.

One way to imagine opportunities for intergenerational giving and serving
is to examine all giving and serving opportunities and practices in the congregation to determine whether and how they can be made more appropriate for multiple generations. Consider these options:

- Integrate young people into existing service or giving activities that the
  congregation sponsors but that have been primarily the domain of adults.
  These might include stewardship campaigns, fund-raising, and service
  or justice activities.
- Engage more adults in existing youth service efforts—not just as driv-
  ers or chaperone, but as coworkers. Young people can invite adults to
  participate with them.
- Form individual or group mentoring relationships between youth and

adults in which one thing they do together is to undertake a service or giving project.

The Unitarian Church of Davenport, Iowa, discovered that active youth involvement in stewardship initiatives could strengthen their efforts. For years, the church had focused on soliciting financial pledges from adults. Then leaders realized that they were leaving out the youth. Now, ten to 15 junior- and senior-high youth work with the adults to raise church funds through a variety of activities and events. In addition, several young people participate in the annual pledge drive by canvassing members of the congregation, asking them to contribute—while building bonds between youth and adults.

Intergenerational service activities provide wonderful opportunities to nurture relationships across all ages. These projects give adults and teenagers who think they don't have anything in common (and may even be afraid of each other) relatively low-risk ways to begin building relationships as they work side by side.

Service and social-action projects most often build intergenerational relationships primarily by recognizing the important role that adult sponsors play in youth service projects and by having young people engage in service with and for senior citizens (such as "Adopt-a-Grandparent" or oral histories). These emphases can be important for nurturing intergenerational relationships. In addition, there is tremendous potential in designing service experiences in which people of all ages—from children and youth to young adults to middle-aged to elderly—serve others together, side by side, reflecting on the experience and its meaning together.

## THE CHALLENGE OF CULTURE CHANGE

These two chapters have presented eight keys and more than 30 specific dimensions whereby congregations nurture giving and serving. That number may seem overwhelming. How do you begin to take steps to strengthen giving and serving in your own congregation?

Given the complexity of culture change and congregational transformation, it is tempting to narrow the scope to tweaking or adding a specific program or curriculum. Yet while this narrow approach may be more comfortable and manageable, it is unlikely, by itself, to have a lasting impact. In his book *The Innovative Church*, Merton P. Strommen, founder of Search Institute, outlines a framework for bringing about lasting change in congregations, based on extensive research on organizational change across several decades. Strommen lists seven key elements of a planning and change process, whose initial letters spell the acronym FUTURES.[39]

### FREE PEOPLE TO PARTICIPATE

This element involves creating a climate of enthusiasm for change, sparking creativity and involvement. For this element to be in place, leaders need to be open, affirming, flexible, and ready to encourage creativity and innovation, rather than seeking to control the process.

### UNITE AROUND NEEDS

An awareness of need is essential to change. "To introduce a change or innovation for which a group has no felt need is to court failure," Strommen writes.[40] This element requires, then, understanding both the current realities for people in the congregation as well as their hopes and dreams—with the hope and possibility becoming clear in the gap between present realities and future hopes.

### TIE INNOVATION TO MISSION AND VALUES

A new idea is unlikely to be adopted if it is not connected to the organization's identity, mission, history, values, or "mental models" that shape how people act.

### USE INPUT OF LEGITIMIZERS

Every congregation includes powerful people whose support—or lack of it—will have a great impact on whether change occurs. While it can be tempting to avoid those who resist change, involving gatekeepers and opinion leaders in the process will both strengthen the change and make it more likely to be accepted and sustained.

## RALLY BROAD OWNERSHIP

The more people who become involved and connected to a new approach, the more likely it is to be successful. Thus it is important to identify the various stakeholders in the congregation and find ways to connect them to your efforts.

## ENGAGE IN ACTION

Don't plan incessantly. Try something. Send up test balloons. Do short-term projects (and reflect on how they go). In a sense, these experiments serve the role of get-going-quick programs and activities. The difference is that they are within the context of a larger vision, direction, and plan.

## SUSTAIN THE INNOVATION LONG-TERM

The key to sustaining the effort is continually to reflect on, learn from, and build on your early efforts. It doesn't mean simply following, lock-step, what you agreed to do a year ago. Strommen writes: "A long-term approach views the launching of an innovation as a continuing process and not a finished act."[41]

Who does this work? While it is often fueled by a key leader or champion, it requires a team with the vision, passion, and commitment to follow it through. Such a team not only spreads the workload, but learns together, reinforces and supports its members, and provides continuity amid the inevitable changes.

## GETTING STARTED

While culture change is long-term and complex, there are concrete ways to begin the process. Here are some starting points to consider:

- *Engage others in the process.* Build an intergenerational team to guide this journey with you.

- *Learn about current realities and dreams.* Check your assumptions and perspectives with people of all ages. Depending on your congregation's culture, you can do this in informal ways (such as conversations) or more formal approaches (focus groups or surveys).
- *Examine traditions, history, and priorities.* Explore what your congregation is in a position to do and become, given your faith tradition and your congregation's own history and identity. Tap the rituals and practices of faith (prayer, study, worship, discernment) to guide the process.
- *Connect with others outside your congregation.* One of the things we have shared in this book is how many congregations of many traditions have developed innovative strategies for addressing giving and serving. Find others in your community, denomination, or other networks that can be a resource for you as you examine these issues and possibilities.[42]
- *Build on current strengths.* These may be strengths and emphases from the past. They may be current activities, relationships, and programs. How can they be strengthened or replicated? (If you start by filling gaps, you can quickly become overwhelmed and discouraged, particularly if filling the gaps is a long-term or resource-intensive process.)
- *Keep the big picture in mind, but do something concrete.* Some people are naturally drawn to long-term, big-picture visions and possibilities. Others want something concrete and practical to do right now. Both perspectives need to be valued. The long-term perspective ensures that short-term activities are moving you incrementally toward a larger vision. The concrete, short-term activities allow you to make progress, have something to celebrate, and give you practice as you continue the journey.
- *Reflect as you go.* While most congregations do not have formal evaluation processes, providing a time for reflection can have the same benefits for your planning as they have for young people in giving and serving. Take time to reflect on what has been done so far, how it is going, and what that means for next steps.
- *Don't expect everything to go as planned.* Some things won't work. Other great things will happen that you didn't even think about. Recognize that any change effort is a learning process and that the plans you set in the beginning won't necessarily match where you end up . . . and that's OK.

Virtually every congregation is already on a journey to nurture generosity in young people. Some may have only a few things in place, such as public requests for volunteers or contributions. Others may already have many of the elements suggested by these eight keys integrated into their congregation. The challenge is not to try to do everything overnight, because long-term culture change doesn't happen that way. The challenge is to discover where you are on the journey and to join with others who are also on the way, discovering what works and what doesn't.

There is no one way for a given congregation to proceed on this journey. But the path of discovery, growth, and learning has great potential for strengthening the congregation and cultivating in young people a lifetime commitment to their congregation and to a life of generosity.

# POSTSCRIPT

An artist creates a mosaic by placing *tesserae*, small pieces of colored glass, stone, or other material, into mortar to create a picture. If you stand up close to the piece of art, it can be difficult to discern the overall pattern. It's only when you step back from the detail that you can see the artist's vision.

In many ways, this book is a mosaic. Some of the *tesserae* are the gems of wisdom from congregational leaders and national experts. Some are the nuggets of stories about how congregations nurture generosity. Some are the various research studies. Because the pieces come from different congregations and faith traditions, each adds its own texture and tone. The pieces are held together by the "mortar" of themes, chapters, and conceptual frameworks.

Up close, it may be difficult to discern overall patterns and designs. But what do you see when you step back? We suggest several themes:

- Today's young people live in a culture that encourages—lures—them to focus only on themselves. And while there is an emphasis on engaging young people in serving others, very little is being done to encourage young people to share their financial resources with others. Such a focus is critical, not only because young people increasingly have and spend more money, but also because financial habits established during childhood and adolescence are likely to continue throughout life.
- If we want young people to grow up generous, we cannot rely on an isolated youth program or curriculum to instill commitments to giving and serving. Such priorities require a web of experiences and relationships that motivate, inspire, expect, and equip young people to give and serve.

- All aspects of congregational life, not just the youth program, can play a role in nurturing generosity in young people. If congregations seek to nurture generous youth, they must continually seek to be generous communities that both nurture a culture and teach the practices of generosity.
- Perhaps the most important and fundamental shift needed is to recognize young people as resources and contributors, not merely adults-in-waiting. Not only will youth benefit when they are encouraged and supported in taking a lead and making a difference, but their energy, commitment, and vision can help to transform the entire congregation.

When you step back, you may see different patterns in the mosaic. You may wish to add different nuances or whole new sections to the picture. You may even think we misplaced some of the pieces—or picked the wrong ones. We invite you to join the creative process. Though we have put our current understanding into print, the mortar that holds these pieces together has not yet set. It is still flexible. We encourage you to pull out pieces, move them around, and see what you create in the process.

And when you do try something, please share it with us. Let us know what works, what doesn't. Send your insights, models, and experiences to:

Eugene C. Roehlkepartain
Search Institute
700 South Third Street, Suite 210
Minneapolis, MN 55415
gener@search-institute.org

We are at a critical place with young people in our congregations and community. Across the country, people are coming together to recognize the ways in which we must all work together to reweave the fabric of community life that creates a web in which young people can grow up healthy, caring, and responsible. Your efforts to instill in youth a lifelong commitment to sharing themselves and their resources with others are a vital part of that process. May it be for you and the young people you touch a journey of discovery, growth, and joy.

# Resources on Youth Giving and Serving in Congregations

One of the things we learned from leaders in congregations is that they are not aware of the many resources now available that address giving and serving with young people. We have gathered a listing of a wide variety of tools and resources available to Christian and Jewish congregations. While the scope and approach of these resources varies widely, you will find helpful tools for your needs. A few notes about this list:

- The resources have been organized into three broad categories: Resources on Giving and Serving (resources that integrate the two themes); Resources on Giving; and Resources on Serving. Within these three categories, we have sorted the resources into Foundational Resources (background information and planning), Curriculum and Teaching Tools (for religious education and small-group learning settings); and Activities (projects and events).

- Whereas the footnotes throughout this book have drawn on research and theoretical sources on giving and serving, this list focuses primarily on practical tools for planning and leading educational and action activities.

- We have focused on resources that directly address giving and serving among middle-school and high-school youth in congregations. Thus we have not included the many available resources on giving and serving among younger children or adults, or resources that do not directly address the congregational setting. Nor have we included broad resources on congregational youth work unless they deal extensively with giving or serving.

- We have included a list of selected organizations and Web sites at the end of the resource listing. These include a number of secular organizations that have valuable information on giving or serving for congregations.

• Resource lists become quickly dated as titles go out of print, publishers change their names, and new materials become available. We have attempted to provide current information as of summer 2000. For updated information, contact the identified publisher. (Most publishers have Web sites that can be located through a standard search engine.)

## RESOURCES ON GIVING AND SERVING

### FOUNDATIONAL RESOURCES

Hancock, Jim. *Compassionate Kids: Practical Ways to Involve Your Students in Mission and Service.* El Cajon, Calif: Youth Specialties, 1995. This book helps youth groups learn about poverty and what they can do about it. It addresses creative giving, deciding what you want to do, resources and organizations that can help you get started, and careers that make a difference.

Roehlkepartain, Eugene C. *Kids Have a Lot to Give: How Congregations Can Nurture Habits of Giving and Serving for the Common Good.* Minneapolis: Search Institute, 1999. A practical guide that challenges congregations to nurture in youth lifelong habits of giving and serving. Introduces eight research-based keys effective in encouraging giving and serving. Shows why giving and serving are important, describes successful programs throughout the country, and provides extensive list of resources.

Sa, Soozung. *Caring From the Inside Out: How to Help Youth Show Compassion.* Nashville: Abingdon, 1997. This book focuses on helping youth leaders assess and develop compassionate behavior in youth. It describes practical and specific ideas for caring, serving, and giving within the congregation and in the larger community.

## CURRICULUM AND TEACHING TOOLS

Grishaver, Joel Lurie, and Beth Huppin. *Tzedakah, Gemilut Chasadim and Ahavah: A Manual for World Repair.* Denver: Alternatives in Religious Education, 1983. This workbook combines a study of Jewish texts with decision-making and reflective activities to help young people integrate traditional teachings with their own beliefs, values, and actions.

Kadden, Barbara Binder, and Bruce Kadden. *Teaching Mitzvot: Concepts, Values and Activities.* Denver: A.R.E. Publishing, 1996. This curriculum includes 36 units that deal with different mitzvot, or obligations, including two units on *tzedakah.*

Siegel, Danny. *Mitzvahs.* Millburn, N.J.: CMS Distributors/Eisenberger, 1995. This book collects short stories and articles on a variety of topics related to mitzvot. It includes stories about *"mitzvah* heroes," descriptions of *tzedakah* projects, and other information.

Summers, Barbara Fortgang. *Community and Responsibility in the Jewish Tradition.* New York: United Synagogue Youth, 1986. This comprehensive curriculum integrates the study of biblical and rabbinical texts on *tzedakah, gemilut hasadim,* and related topics with reflection and discussion about group members' beliefs, values and behaviors towards others.

## ACTIVITIES

Isaacs, Ronald H., and Kerry M. Olitzy. *Doing Mitzvot: Mitzvah Projects for Bar/Bat Mitzvah.* Hoboken, N.J.: KTAV Publishing, 1994. This book describes opportunities for mitzvot every month during the bar or bat mitzvah year. Each unit focuses on a mitzvah and includes the history, related texts, discussion questions, the month's project, a journal page, and resources for further study.

Roehlkepartain, Jolene L. *Teaching Kids to Care and Share.* Nashville: Abingdon, 2000. This book is a collection of more than 300 serving and giving activities for children and young adolescents. It also includes numerous handouts to support learning activities.

Siegel, Danny. *116 Practical Mitzvah Suggestions.* New York: United Synagogue Youth, 1995. This booklet highlights 116 practical ideas for mitzvah projects.

## Resources on Giving

### Foundational Resources

Burkett, Larry. *Finances for Children and Teenagers.* Gainesville, Ga.: Christian Financial Concepts, 1995. This booklet helps parents teach children about finances and money management based on biblical principles from an evangelical Christian perspective.

Epstein, Jerome M. *Tzedakah: A Matter of Priorities.* New York: United Synagogue Youth, n.d. This booklet applies Jewish traditions and teachings to contemporary needs in Jewish communities.

Roehlkepartain, Jolene L. *An Asset Builder's Guide to Youth and Money.* Minneapolis: Search Institute, 1999. This workbook helps youth and y couth leaders explore their beliefs and values about money and develop financial skills and competencies based on their own values and priorities. It is desgined for use in congregations and other youth-serving settings.

Ronsvalle, John and Sylvia, with U. Milo Kaufmann. *At Ease: Discussing Money and Values in Small Groups.* Bethesda: Alban Institute, 1998. This book offers practical ways to introduce issues of money and giving to small groups in Christian churches.

Siegel, Danny. *Tzedakah: Jewish Giving—A Privilege.* New York: United Synagogue Youth, n.d. This booklet weaves together texts, traditions, and inspiring stories to enrich young people's understanding of *tzedakah* and *gemilut chassadim.*

Swartz, Rita McCarthy. *Stewardship Programs for Children and Youth.* Kansas City, Mo.: Sheed & Ward, 1996. This manual provides step-by-step information about how to develop a stewardship program for youth, including information for involving parents.

Vincent, Mark. *Teaching a Christian View of Money: Celebrating God's Generosity.* Scottdale, Pa.: Herald Press, 1997. This book and planning guide challenges Christian congregations to think of money and stewardship as a faith response, not fund-raising. It offers Bible studies and practical strategies for strengthening stewardship efforts.

## CURRICULUM AND TEACHING TOOLS

*Beyond the News: Money.* Harrisonburg, Va.: Mennonite Media/Mennonite Board of Missions, 1997. This video promotes discussion about the decisions we make about money, including issues of values, stewardship, consumption, and giving. A study guide includes Scriptures and discussion questions.

Burkett, L. Allen, and Lauree Burkett. *Money Matters for Teens.* Chicago: Moody Press, 1997. This book (and accompanying workbooks for ages 11 to 14 and ages 15 to 18) teaches teenagers biblical principles of stewardship and financial management from an evangelical Christian perspective. It addresses saving, investing, loans, checking accounts, and credit cards.

Cain, Carolyn E. *Come Aboard the Steward Ship.* New York: Office of Stewardship, Episcopal Church (USA), 1990. This set of five booklets (for grades K-12) teaches about sharing time, talent, and treasure. It also includes family stewardship activities and an activity to assess individual talents.

Chase, Robert. *Ever Expanding Circles: A Stewardship Video Curriculum for Youth.* Louisville: Stewardship Education, Presbyterian Church (USA), n.d. This multimedia presentation teaches young adolescents how stewardship relates to their daily lives.

Cross, Marie T., and Beth Basham, eds. *Choices: Living and Learning in God's World–Youth Education Packet.* Louisville: Presbyterian Church (U.S.A.), 1997. This comprehensive stewardship education program introduces Christian stewardship to youth and their families. It includes eight study guides, a game, a personal journal, and other tools.

De Vries, Robert, et al. *Gotta Have It: It's a Stewardship Thing.* Grand Rapids: CRC Publications, 1995. This four-lesson curriculum (with a leader's guide and student handbook) for youth groups focuses on money management and stewardship from a Christian perspective.

Dick, Dan R. *Choices and Challenges: Stewardship Strategies for Youth.* Nashville: Discipleship Resources, 1994. This collection of lesson plans for Christian youth groups addresses stewardship of time, money, relationships, and possessions in today's world.

Duerksen, Carol. *Living Beyond Our Means: The Extravagance of Biblical Stewardship.* Newton, Kans.: Faith and Life Press/Brethren Press,

1996. This curriculum challenges youth to make choices and commitments based on a Christian understanding of stewardship.

*Lifestyles of the Rich and Faithful: A Stewardship Education Resource
for Youth.* Chicago: Evangelical Lutheran Church in America Division
for Congregational Ministries—Youth Ministries, 1993. This seven-ses-
sion curriculum addresses stewardship, discovering your gifts, decision-making, and related topics.

*Parents' Guide to Teaching Youth to Share.* Minneapolis: Lutheran Brotherhood, 2000. This small booklet provides basic information for parents
about how to talk with children about managing and sharing their money
from a Christian perspective.

Perron, Bob. *The Stewardship Game.* Kansas City, Mo.: Sheed & Ward,
1997. This board game teaches young people about choices they can
make every day to be good stewards of time, talent, and treasure.
Players draw cards with examples of good or bad stewardship or read-
aloud Bible verses about stewardship.

Rusbuldt, Richard E. *A Workbook on Biblical Stewardship.* Grand Rapids: Eerdmans, 1994. This leader's guide and workbook contrast the
ownership model of stewardship with a Christian model of "care-man-
agement."

Salkin, Jeffrey K. *Putting God on the Guest List: How to Reclaim the
Spiritual Meaning of Your Child's Bar or Bat Mitzvah,* 2nd edition.
Woodstock, Vt.: Jewish Lights, 1996. This book offers creative ideas
to make bar or bat mitzvah more meaningful, including extensive information to encourage young people to make *tzedakah* part of their
celebration. An edition is also available for young people themselves.

Vincent, Mark, and Dale Shenk. *The Link . . . Better to Give: A Study on
Stewardship/Hope for the Future.* Scottdale, Pa.: Herald Press, 1997.
This curriculum teaches Christian beliefs, values, and traditions about
money, helping teens relate their personal values and faith to giving.

*Young Stewards in Formation.* Wichita, Kans.: Catholic Archdiocese of
Wichita, 1996. This Roman Catholic curriculum presents stewardship
as a way of life for students in grades K-12.

### ACTIVITIES

Siegel, Danny. *An Invitation: Jewish Collectibles.* New York: United Synagogue Youth, n.d. This booklet challenges young people to use bar or bat mitzvah as an opportunity to share with those in need around the world.

*World Vision 30-Hour Famine: Feed the Need.* Tacoma, Wash.: World Vision 30-Hour Famine, 1999. This kit offers plans and tools for leading this hunger awareness and fund-raising youth event in a church.

Zentner, Mary Ingram, ed. *The Real Meal Deal Planning Guide.* Chicago: Evangelical Lutheran Church in America, 1997. This kit provides resources for planning and leading a fund-raising retreat that addresses world hunger.

## RESOURCES ON SERVING

### FOUNDATIONAL RESOURCES

Benson, Peter L., and Eugene C. Roehlkepartain. *Beyond Leaf Raking: Learning to Serve/Serving to Learn.* Nashville: Abingdon, 1993. This comprehensive guide to service-learning in Christian congregations emphasizes the importance of planning and reflection in ensuring that youth service contributes to young people's personal and spiritual development.

Moseley, Michael, and John Roberto. *Youthworks*, revised edition. Naugatuck, Conn.: Center for Ministry Development, 1996. This multivolume resource set provides extensive materials for all aspects of a comprehensive youth ministry (from a Catholic perspective), including detailed information on integrating service and justice issues into youth ministry.

Roberto, John. *Family Works.* Naugatuck, Conn.: Center for Ministry Development, 1995. This comprehensive resource for strengthening the partnership between the family and the Catholic parish includes extensive information on planning family service and justice activities.

Roehlkepartain, Eugene C., Thomas Bright, and Beth Margolis-Rupp. *An Asset Builder's Guide to Service-Learning.* Minneapolis: Search Institute, 2000. This guide provides practical tools for planning and implementing service-learning in a congregation or other youth-serving setting based on Search Institute's framework of developmental assets.

## Curriculum and Teaching Tools

Bayar, Steven. *To Fix the World—Stick Your Neck Out.* Millburn, N.J.: Ziv Tzedakah Fund, 1998. Developed with the Giraffe Project (see organizations below), this curriculum integrates social action with Jewish teachings and themes.

Gritter-Dykstra, Michelle. *Living the Lord's Prayer* (student and leader's book). Grand Rapids: CRC Publications, 1995. This curriculum combines study of the Lord's Prayer with team-based service projects. It includes a student journal and emphasizes reflection and connecting service with faith tradition.

Robinson, Ron. *The All-Purpose Youth Service Kit.* Nashville: Cokesbury, 1996. This guide includes five sessions on service and servanthood to prepare Christian youth groups for service-learning experiences. A Servant Journal is also available that provides a structure for young people to reflect on ten days of service.

Siegel, Danny. *Gym Shoes and Irises (Personalized Tzedakah)—Book Two.* Millburn, N.J.: CMS Distributors/Eisenberger, 1987. This book is a primer on *tzedakah*, including introductions to Jewish ethics, practical suggestions for action and stories of "mitzvah heroes."

———. *Heroes and Miracle Workers.* Millburn, N.J.: CMS Distributors/Eisenberger, 1997. This book is another collection of inspiring stories about "mitzvah heroes."

Tamsberg, Kathy. *Pursuing Justice: A Social Justice Curriculum for Churches.* Washington: Alliance of Baptists, 1999. This curriculum helps students link their spiritual life and traditions to social justice. The sessions include Bible readings, music, lists of resources and organizations, and suggested activities for a wide variety of justice-related topics.

Turnbull, Helen, and Debbie Gowensmith. *Faith on Fire: 15 Lessons to Help Teenagers Change the World.* Loveland, Co.: Group Books, 1999. These 15 lessons connect the Christian faith with service to others, including stewardship of the environment, service to the community, and service in the world.

*Under Construction: A Habitat for Humanity Vacation Bible School Curriculum.* Macon, Ga.: Smyth & Helwys, 1999. This Christian education resource uses a construction metaphor to teach children the value of service in an active, engaging setting.

Woods, Paul. *Serving Your Neighbors.* Loveland, Co.: Group Publishing, 1994. This four-week curriculum for Christian youth groups focuses on service and servanthood.

## ACTIVITIES

Case, Steven, and Fred Cornforth. *Hands-On Service Ideas for Youth Groups.* Loveland, Colo.: Group Publishing, 1995. This collection of 102 service project ideas for Christian youth groups begins with "Adopt-a-Grandparent" and ends with "Youth to Youth."

Siegel, Danny. *11 Ways USYers Can Change the World in Big Ways Or: How to Put Your Mitzvah Power Hungriness to Work.* New York: United Synagogue Youth, n.d.. This practical pamphlet outlines the steps involved in 11 mitzvah projects that youth groups can do.

*The Social Action Ideas Handbook.* New York: United Synagogue Youth, n.d.. This handbook helps youth groups design social action programs. It describes a wide variety of projects within the synagogue and in the wider community.

## ORGANIZATIONS AND WEB SITES

Christian Financial Concepts, Box 2458, Gainesville, GA 30503; (770) 534-1000; http://cfcministry.org. Founded by Larry Burkett, CFC is the premier evangelical organization focused on financial management. Its Web site includes a wide range of information and financial planning tools. A spin-off organization, Larry Burkett's Money Matters for Kids (www.mmforkids.org), provides information to help parents, children, and teenagers "understand the biblical principles of stewardship."

Corporation for National Service, 1201 New York Ave. NW, Washington, DC 20525; (202) 606-5000; www.cns.gov. The corporation sponsors Learn and Serve America, which supports service-learning projects in schools. Its Web site includes extensive news about the history of and federal support for youth service, and the Learn and Serve America section lists service-learning contacts in all 50 states.

Do Something, 423 W. 55th St., 8th Floor, New York, NY 10019; (212) 523-1175; www.dosomething.org. Founded on the belief that positive change is possible and that young people have the power to create that change, Do Something offers a variety of national programs to inspire young people to action, including the annual BRICK Award for Community Leadership, which honors young leaders who are rebuilding community.

Giraffe Project, Box 759, 197 Second St., Langley, WA 98260; (360) 221-7989; www.giraffe.org. Dedicated to encouraging people to "stick their necks out for the common good," this organization produces materials and shares stories and quotations through its Web site to motivate people to help others and build community.

Global Youth Action Network, 211 E. 43rd St., Suite 905, New York, NY 10017; (212) 661-6111; www.youthlink.org. This international collaboration of youth and youth-serving organizations (and the U.S. network Youth in Action) seeks to promote greater youth engagement and more opportunities for young people to be heard through national and global youth agendas. The youthlink.org Web site includes a variety of tools and links for youth empowerment.

Independent Sector, 1200 18th St. NW, Suite 200, Washington, DC 20036; (202) 223-8100; www.independentsector.org. Independent Sector is engaged in significant research and leadership on U.S. philanthropy. The Web site provides access to extensive research on giving and serving among American adults and youth, based on the organization's latest national surveys.

International Youth Hall of Fame, 300 Queen Anne Ave. N. #201, Seattle, WA 98109; (206) 623-6770; www.youthhall.org. This organization supports local chapters that recognize young people who are "making a positive difference at home, in school, and in the community."

Jump$tart Coalition for Personal Financial Literacy, 919 18th St. NW, Suite 300, Washington, DC 20006; (888) 45-EDUCATE; www.jumpstartcoalition.org. The Jump$tart Coalition promotes financial literacy among young people through research, advocacy, and maintaining (with the National Institute for Consumer Education) a Web-based Personal Finance Clearinghouse.

National Charities Information Bureau, 19 Union Square W.; New York, NY 10003; (212) 929-6300; www.give.org. This site promotes well-informed giving by people of all ages by providing a free guide to responsible giving and quick reference information on hundreds of charities.

National Service-Learning Clearinghouse, University of Minnesota, Dept. of Work, Community & Family Education, 1954 Buford Ave., Room R-460, St. Paul, MN 55108; (800) 808-7378; www.nicsl.coled.umn.edu. Funded by the Corporation for National Service, this comprehensive site focuses on all dimensions of service-learning, covering kindergarten through higher education. It includes a comprehensive database on service-learning.

National Youth Leadership Council, 1910 West County Road B, St. Paul, MN 55113; (651) 631-3672; www.nylc.org. NYLC is a pioneer organization in service-learning and youth leadership, particularly in public schools. It provides extensive resources and training as well as hosting an annual service-learning conference.

Points of Light Foundation, 1400 I St. NW, Suite 800, Washington, DC 20005 (202) 729-8000; www.pointsoflight.org. This high-visibility organization offers a variety of resources, programs, and activities related to service, including a variety of youth service programs and resources, the Family Matters program (which focuses on family volunteerism), and Seasons of Service (which highlights days of service throughout the year).

Search Institute, 700 S. Third St., Suite 210, Minneapolis, MN 55415; 800-888-7828; www.search-institute.org. This nonprofit organization focuses on research and education on the healthy development of children and youth and on how institutions and communities support positive development. It offers a variety of tools and resources for congregations, schools, and other organizations.

Tzedakah, Inc., Box 34947, West Bethesda, MD 20827; (800) 448-3107; http://just-tzedakah.org. This organization's Web site provides extensive information on Jewish giving, including guidelines for giving from traditional sources, descriptions of Jewish charities, and information on electronic giving.

USY Social Action and Tikkun Olam, Rapaport House, 155 Fifth Ave., New York NY 10010-6802; (212) 533-7800; www.uscj.org/usy/sato. SATO is a youth-led group within United Synagogue Youth dedicated to social action. The Web site allows members of USY to learn and talk about their commitment to serving and giving. It includes a program bank and a publication list with lots of ideas for action.

Youth Ministry Central, Youth Specialties, Box 22005, El Cajon, CA 92022; (619) 440-2333; www.youthspecialties.com/central. This comprehensive Web site on Christian youth ministry includes a forum for discussing missions and service in youth ministry as well as a listing of Christian missions and service organizations.

Youth Service America, 1101 15th St. NW, Suite 200, Washington, DC 20005; (202) 296-2992; www.ysa.org. Youth Service America is a resource center and alliance of more than 200 organizations "committed to increasing the quantity and quality of opportunities for young Americans to serve locally, nationally, or globally." Among its many initiatives is www.servenet.org, a major Web site on service and volunteering that includes a database of service opportunities across the United States.

# Profiles of Highlighted Congregations

L eaders from the following churches and synagogues provided in-depth information on youth giving and serving in their congregations, through telephone interviews in summer and fall 1999. The congregations were selected through a nomination process in which leaders in various faith traditions and other contacts in the field recommended congregations that they believed were effectively addressing giving or serving with young people. Preliminary interviews with more than 100 congregations provided additional information for selecting these congregations. The information below was current at the time of the interview.

## THE CONGREGATIONS

*Ankeny Presbyterian Church, Ankeny, Iowa.* This primarily Anglo congregation of 350 members north of Des Moines has a small, active youth group, which is involved in giving and serving throughout the year, with young people initiating many of the projects. Through a partnership with an inner-city church, the youth work with young people from the partner congregation to lead a summer recreation program and an after-school program. The congregation is affiliated with the Presbyterian Church (U.S.A.).

*Anshei Emeth Memorial Congregation, New Brunswick, N.J.* Social action is woven into all youth events at this synagogue of 600 families. The goal of this emphasis is to nurture young people so that a commitment to *tikkun olam* becomes an integral part of their Jewish identity. Among many other activities, high school youth participate in four-day training in Washington, D.C., devoted to social activism inspired by

Jewish ethical teachings. The congregation is affiliated with the Union
   of American Hebrew Congregations.

*Beth Jacob Congregation, Mendota Heights, Minn.* This congregation
   of 350 families has an active commitment to engaging young people—
   and the whole congregation—in giving and serving. For example, a
   donation of 3 percent of the proceeds from paid-for events is sent to
   Mazone, a Jewish hunger relief organization. Young people are active
   in leading all youth programming (including establishing a budget) and
   serving in and through the congregation. The congregation is affiliated
   with the United Synagogue of Conservative Judaism.

*Congregation Kehilath Jeshurun, New York, N.Y.* This congregation of
   1,000 families with 1,250 in religious school encourages giving beginning in the nursery and continuing throughout life. Children and youth
   (across all grades) also maintain a year-around toy drive by regularly
   donating an unopened birthday gift to the fund. B'nei mitzvah students
   donate a portion of their gift proceeds to the social-action fund of the
   synagogue. The congregation is affiliated with the Orthodox Union.

*Fellowship Evangelical Free Church, Knoxville, Tenn.* This congregation of 2,800 members and 250 junior and senior high youth engages
   young people in a wide range of short- and long-term service-learning
   projects. The mostly white congregation has also created a partnership with an inner-city African-American church that leads to a variety of cooperative projects. The congregation is affiliated with the
   Evangelical Free Church of America.

*First Chinese Baptist Church, San Francisco, Calif.* This 500-member
   congregation of Chinese-Americans places a strong emphasis on developing young people's leadership skills and their commitment to serving
   in the community, including a major, youth-led summer program for
   children. Many of the congregation's giving and serving activities reflect the high value the congregation places on generations valuing and
   respecting each other. The congregation is affiliated with the American Baptist Churches in the U.S.A.

*Ginghamsburg United Methodist Church, Tipp City, Ohio.* The youth
   ministry is the primary force behind this 1,200-member congregation's
   missions ministry, which includes outreach into nearby Dayton. The
   young people plan and lead numerous service activities throughout the
   year, including several service trips. The youth group is actively involved in planning and building a teen nightclub called "Planet Soul."

The mostly white congregation is affiliated with the United Methodist Church.

*Greater St. James Fire Baptized Holiness Church, Detroit, Mich.* This 180-member congregation with 30 teenagers has a strong commitment to strengthening its community. The church emphasizes intergenerational connections and engages young people in leadership and mentoring for younger children. The youth group often plans activities to include children from the community. The congregation is affiliated with the Fire Baptized Holiness Church of the God of the Americas.

*Heritage Baptist Church, Cartersville, Ga.* This 450-member, mostly white congregation northwest of Atlanta has high expectations that children and youth will be involved in giving and serving. This youth group emphasizes developing ongoing relationships with the people they serve, including relationships with children from a local shelter. The youth are partners with adults in stewardship and service projects. The congregation is affiliated with the Alliance of Baptists and the Cooperative Baptist Fellowship.

*Jewish Reconstructionist Congregation, Evanston, Ill.* This congregation with 450 households is using social action programs to build interest in youth group participation. Service is integrated throughout congregational life, not the responsibility of a single committee. The congregation focuses on building an active core of youth leaders who can act as spokespersons and peer mentors. The congregation is affiliated with the Jewish Reconstructionist Federation.

*Kehilat Israel, Pacific Palisades, Calif.* The synagogue integrates *tikkun olam* into all its youth curricula, with an emphasis on weaving Torah and history around young people's needs and concerns, not vice versa. Young people are also encouraged to be mentors for younger children. (For example, b'nei mitzvah students research a cause and publicize it among younger grades to encourage giving.) The congregation is affiliated with the Jewish Reconstructionist Federation.

*Kirkwood Baptist Church, Kirkwood, Mo.* Young people take the lead in several congregationwide service activities in this 1,100-member, mostly white congregation in suburban St. Louis. Building and maintaining relationships with people and communities that are served is emphasized; thus, many of the congregation's activities involve returning to the same communities or neighborhoods year after year. The congregation is affiliated with the Cooperative Baptist Fellowship.

*Mount Zion Temple, St. Paul, Minn.* Young people have active leadership roles in this temple of 750 families. Youth group members sit on the congregation's board of trustees and other planning committees, and a youth-run leadership team coordinates all youth programming. The congregation is affiliated with the Union of American Hebrew Congregations.

*Netarts Friends Congregation, Tillamook, Ore.* The 15 young people in this 50-member, white congregation on the Oregon coast initiate and lead many giving and serving activities. Rarely are young people asked to lead; they volunteer to lead based on their own strengths and talents. The congregation is affiliated with the Northwest Yearly Meeting of Friends, Society of Friends.

*Our Savior's Lutheran Church, Box Elder, Mont.* This 190-member Native American congregation emphasizes youth service despite the many economic and social struggles the youth face. The young people plan and implement most of the giving and serving projects. Among the projects young people have done are projects to help elders, hospice patients, and residents of a local chemical dependency treatment center. The congregation is affiliated with the Evangelical Lutheran Church in America.

*Sinai Temple, Springfield, Mass.* Humor and creativity inspire enthusiastic youth participation in giving and serving projects in this synagogue that includes 600 families. For instance, Rabbi Mark Shapiro regularly paints a fund-raising needle on the seat of his pants so that everyone can monitor how a giving campaign is going. Synagogue youth are encouraged to participate in a citywide trust fund that enables them to designate monies to a number of local Jewish organizations. The congregation is affiliated with the Union of American Hebrew Congregations.

*St. John's Cathedral, Albuquerque, N.M.* This mostly white, 1,000-member congregation engages young people in a variety of short- and long-term service projects with other Episcopal congregations as well as congregations from other faith traditions. There is a strong emphasis in developing leadership skills in all youth group activities. The congregation is affiliated with the Episcopal Church.

*St. Michael's Catholic Church, Stillwater, Minn.* The mostly white, 2,400-member congregation sponsors a youth group of 475 youth, which includes young people from the nearby St. Mary's Catholic Church. Young people choose, plan, lead, and participate in short- and long-term service projects throughout the year, including an intensive summer program that includes weekly projects. An effort is made to provide a wide range of age-appropriate activities and experiences. The congregation is affiliated with the Roman Catholic Church.

*Temple Israel, Minneapolis, Minn.* This congregation of 2,100 adult members requires all seventh and eighth graders to do at least 25 hours of community service. Personal inventories are used to match students' interests with individualized projects. A Friday night service at the end of the school year honors student achievements in service areas and other aspects of congregational life. The congregation is affiliated with the Union of American Hebrew Congregations.

*Tifereth Israel Congregation, Columbus, Ohio.* This congregation of 1,300 families (and 100 youth in youth group) seeks to build community among young people before engaging them in social action. Youth participate in a social-action training program in Washington, D.C., as the culminating event to a course on tikkun olam and social action. The congregation is affiliated with the United Synagogue of Conservative Judaism.

## HABITS OF THE HEART CONGREGATIONS IN INDIANA

In addition to the congregations interviewed across the United States, we also learned from the congregations that were involved in Habits of the Heart in Indiana. They were Catholic Community of the Sacred Heart, Jeffersonville; Fairview Presbyterian Church, Indianapolis; First Friends Meeting, Richmond; Mount Zion Baptist Church, Indianapolis; St. Augustine Catholic Church, Jeffersonville; and Temple Adath B'nai Israel, Evansville.

## YOUTH FOCUS GROUP

The following congregations and organizations hosted focus groups with young people from congregations in fall 1999. In most cases, a leader from the congregation led the discussion, using a focus-group protocol developed by Search Institute. Each session was recorded and transcribed.

- Indiana Humanities Council, Indianapolis, Indiana (youth from two Christian congregations)
- Seventh and James Baptist Church, Waco, Texas
- Jewish Community Relations Council, St. Paul, Minn. (youth from two Jewish congregations)
- St. Anthony's Catholic Church, Hot Springs, S. Dak.

**Introduction**

1. From the Web site of the K-12 Education in Philanthropy Project: www.msu.edu/~k12phil/.

2. John Ronsvalle and Sylvia Ronsvalle, "Giving to Religion: How Generous Are We?" *The Christian Century* (June 3-10, 1998), 579-581.

3. Lloyd D. Johnston, Jerald G. Bachman, and Patrick M. O'Malley, *Monitoring the Future: Questionnaire Responses from the Nation's High School Seniors, 1995* (Ann Arbor: Survey Research Center, Institute for Social Research, University of Michigan, 1997), 199-201.

4. Virginia A. Hodgkinson and Murray S. Weitzman, *Volunteering and Giving among Teenagers 12 to 17 Years of Age: Findings from a National Survey,* 1996 edition (Washington: Independent Sector, 1997), 18, 67.

**Chapter 1**

1. From the Web site of the Religious Action Center of Reform Judaism: www.rj.org/rac/social/additionalyth.html

2. Mary J. Oates, *The Catholic Philanthropic Tradition in America* (Bloomington, Ind.: Indiana University Press, 1995), 168.

3. Virginia A. Hodgkinson and Murray S. Weitzman, *Volunteering and Giving among Teenagers 12 to 17 Years of Age: Findings from a National Survey,* 1996 edition (Washington: Independent Sector, 1997), 19. See also Dean R. Hoge, Charles Zech, Patrick McNamara, and Michael J. Donahue, *Money Matters: Personal Giving in American Churches* (Louisville: Westminster John Knox, 1996), 55; and Richard J. Bentley and Luana G. Nissan, *The Roots of Giving and Serving: A Literature Review Studying How School-Age Children Learn the Philanthropic Tradition* (Indianapolis: Indiana University Center on Philanthropy, 1996), 56.

4. We recognize that all major world religions (including many that are growing rapidly in the United States) include a strong commitment to giving and serving. However, for a variety of practical reasons (including the shared heritage, similar

polity, and available research), this book focuses on Jewish and Christian traditions.

5. These summaries are only suggestive of the theological and historical themes within these traditions. They capture neither the richness of each tradition nor the significant variation within each tradition. For a more comprehensive examination of the issues for these and other religious traditions, see Robert Wuthnow, Virginia A. Hodgkinson, et al., *Faith and Philanthropy in America: Exploring the Role of Religion in America's Voluntary Sector* (San Francisco: Jossey-Bass, 1990); Warren F. Ilchman, Stanley N. Katz, and Edward L. Queen II, eds., *Philanthropy in the World's Traditions* (Bloomington, Ind.: Indiana University Press, 1998); and Charles H. Hamilton and Warren F. Ilchman, eds., *Cultures of Giving: How Region and Religion Influence Philanthropy* (San Francisco: Jossey-Bass, 1995).

6. Rami M. Shapiro, *Minyan: Ten Principles for Living a Life of Integrity* (New York: Bell Tower, 1997), 114.

7. Mordechai Rimor and Gary A. Tobin, "Jewish Giving Patterns to Jewish and Non-Jewish Philanthropy," in Wuthnow, Hodgkinson, et al., *Faith and Philanthropy in America*, 134, 158.

8. James Hudnut-Beumler, "Protestants and Giving: The Tithes that Bind?" in Hamilton and Ilchman, eds., *Cultures of Giving*, 81.

9. See James R. Wood, "Liberal Protestant Social Action in a Period of Decline," in Wuthnow, Hodgkinson, et al., *Faith and Philanthropy in America*, 165-186.

10. Timothy T. Clydesdale, "Soul-Winning and Social Work: Giving and Caring in the Evangelical Tradition," in Wuthnow, Hodgkinson, et al., *Faith and Philanthropy in America*, 187-210.

11. Ibid., 189.

12. Ibid., 194.

13. Quoted in Clydesdale, "Soul-Winning and Social Work," 197.

14. John E. Tropman, "The Catholic Ethic and the Protestant Ethic," in Paul G. Schervish et al., eds., *Caring and Community in Modern Society: Passing on the Tradition of Service to Future Generations* (San Francisco: Jossey-Bass, 1995), 271.

15. For an in-depth review of the history of Roman Catholic philanthropy in the United States, see Oates, *The Catholic Philanthropic Tradition in America*.

16. National Conference of Catholic Bishops, *Communities of Salt and Light: Reflections on the Social Mission of the Parish* (Washington, D.C.: U.S. Catholic Conference, 1994), 3.

17. William E. McManus, "Stewardship and Almsgiving in the Roman Catholic Tradition," in Wuthnow, Hodgkinson, et al., *Faith and Philanthropy in America*, 124.

18. National Conference of Catholic Bishops, *Stewardship: A Disciple's Response* (Washington: U.S. Catholic Conference, 1993), 34.

19. Oates, *Catholic Philanthropic Tradition*, 166-67.

20. C. Eric Lincoln and Lawrence H. Mamiya, *The Black Church in the African American Experience* (Durham, N.C.: Duke University Press, 1990), 238.

21. Emmett D. Carson, "Patterns of Giving in Black Churches," in Wuthnow, Hodgkinson, et al., *Faith and Philanthropy in America,* 234.

22. Cheryl Hall-Russell and Robert H. Kasberg, *African American Traditions of Giving and Serving: A Midwest Perspective* (Indianapolis: Indiana University Center on Philanthropy, 1997), 10.

23. Ibid., 13.

24. Kenda Creasy Dean and Ron Foster, *The Godbearing Life: The Art of Soul Tending for Youth Ministry* (Nashville: Upper Room, 1998), 107-108.

25. Michael Lerner, *Jewish Renewal: A Path to Healing and Transformation* (New York: Putnam, 1994), 292-93.

26. Nancy Leffert and Hayim Herring, *Shema: Listening to Jewish Youth* (Minneapolis: Search Institute, 1998), 55.

27. Robert Wuthnow, *God and Mammon in America* (New York: Free Press, 1994), 149, 151.

28. For a more comprehensive review of the research on service-learning, see Alan S. Waterman, ed., *Service-Learning: Applications from the Research* (Mahwah, N.J.: Lawrence Erlbaum 1997). See also Robin Vue-Benson, Robert Shumer, and Madeleine S. Hengel, *Impacts and Effects of Service Topic Bibliography* (St. Paul, Minn.: National Service-Learning Cooperative Clearinghouse, University of Minnesota, 1997).

29. Peter L. Benson et al., *A Fragile Foundation: The State of Developmental Assets Among American Youth* (Minneapolis: Search Institute, 1999), 23.

30. George H. Gallup, Jr., *The Spiritual Life of Young Americans: Approaching the Year 2000* (Princeton, N.J.: George H. Gallup International Institute, n.d.), 94-95.

31. Peter L. Benson and Eugene C. Roehlkepartain, *Beyond Leaf Raking: Learning to Serve/Serving to Learn* (Nashville: Abingdon, 1993), 27.

32. Bryan T. Froehle, *New Directions in Catholic Youth Ministry: A National Study of Catholic Youth Ministry Program Participants—Executive Summary* (Washington: Center for Applied Research in the Apostolate, 1996), 6.

33. Hodgkinson and Weitzman, *Volunteering and Giving among Teenagers 12 to 17 Years of Age,* 1996 edition (Washington: Independent Sector, 1997), 37.

34. Danny Siegel, "An Invitation to Jewish Collectibles" (New York: United Synagogue Youth, United Synagogue of Conservative Judaism, n.d.), 7.

35. Peter C. Scales and Nancy Leffert, *Developmental Assets: A Synthesis of the Scientific Research on Adolescent Development* (Minneapolis: Search Institute, 1999).

36. Thomas H. Jeavons, *Cultivating a Critical Compassion: Nurturing the Roots of Philanthropy* (Indianapolis: Indiana University Center on Philanthropy, 1994), 4.

37. William Damon, *Greater Expectations: Overcoming the Culture of Indulgence in Our Homes and Schools* (New York: Free Press, 1995), 157.

38. Ibid., 157-58.

**Chapter 2**

1. Robert Wuthnow, *Rethinking Materialism: Perspectives on the Spiritual Dimension of Economic Behavior* (Grand Rapids: Eerdmans, 1995), 3.

2. This estimate is based on Teenage Research Unlimited's estimate that the average teenager has $86 of weekly income and Independent Sector's survey findings on levels of giving among teenagers and adults. See Peter Zollo, *Wise Up to Teens: Insights into Marketing and Advertising to Teenagers,* 2nd edition (Ithaca, N.Y.: New Strategist Publications, 1999), 8; and Virginia A. Hodgkinson and Murray S. Weitzman, *Volunteering and Giving among Teenagers 12 to 17 Years of Age: Findings from a National Survey,* 1996 edition (Washington: Independent Sector, 1997), 16-17, 86.

3. Jolene L. Roehlkepartain, *An Asset Builder's Guide to Youth and Money* (Minneapolis: Search Institute, 1999), 1. Used with permission of Search Institute.

4. See, for example: Kennon L. Callahan, *Giving and Stewardship in an Effective Church: A Guide for Every Member* (San Francisco: Jossey-Bass, 1992); *Trends in American Jewish Philanthropy: Market Research Analysis* (San Francisco: Center for Modern Jewish Studies, 1992); and Michael Durall, *Creating Congregations of Generous People* (Bethesda: Alban Institute, 1999).

5. See, for example, Virginia A. Hodgkinson and Murray S. Weitzman, *Giving and Volunteering in the United States: Findings from a National Survey,* 1992 edition (Washington: Independent Sector, 1992), 63; and Dean R. Hoge et al., *Money Matters: Personal Giving in American Churches* (Louisville: Westminster John Knox, 1996), 62.

6. These updated estimates from TRU are from "Teens Spend $153 Billion in 1999," press release from Teenage Research Unlimited, Northbrook, Ill. (Oct. 1999).

7. Zollo, *Wise Up to Teens,* 8, 98-99, 14, 228.

8. Dan S. Acuff with Robert H. Reiher, *What Kids Buy and Why: The Psychology of Marketing to Kids* (New York: Free Press, 1997), 1.

9. U.S. Census Bureau, *Poverty in the United States: 1998* (Washington: U.S. Department of Commerce, 1998), v.

10. Zollo, *Wise Up to Teens,* 336.

11. These include the Jump$tart Coalition for Personal Financial Literacy, the National Center for Financial Literacy, and the National Endowment for Financial Education.

12. "Personal Finance Education Guidelines and Benchmarks," www.jumpstartcoalition.org

13. *High School Financial Planning Program Information Kit* (Englewood, Colo.: National Endowment for Financial Education, 1997).

14. *Youth and Money 1999: Results of the 1999 Youth and Money Survey* (Washington: American Savings Education Council, 1999).

15. www.girlsinc.org

16. See, for example, *Parents' Guide to Teaching Youth to Share* (Minneapolis: Lutheran Brotherhood, 2000).

17. *Money Matters in the Millennium* (New York: Merrill Lynch, n.d.).

18. See, for example, Neale S. Godfrey and Carolina Edwards, *Money Doesn't Grow on Trees: A Parent's Guide to Raising Financially Responsible Children* (New York: Fireside, 1994); and Steve Otfinoski, *The Kid's Guide to Money: Earning It, Saving It, Spending It, Growing It, Sharing It* (New York: Scholastic, 1996).

19. Robert Wuthnow, *God and Mammon in America* (New York: Free Press, 1994), 119.

20. Dean R. Hoge et al., *Money Matters: Personal Giving in American Churches* (Louisville: Westminster John Knox, 1996), 11-15.

21. Wesley K. Willmer, "Evangelicals: Linking Fervency of Faith and Generosity of Giving," in Charles H. Hamilton and Warren F. Ilchman, eds., *Cultures of Giving: How Region and Religion Influence Philanthropy* (San Francisco: Jossey-Bass, 1995), 101-115. Also see Hoge et al., *Money Matters.*

22. Gary A. Tobin and Adam Z. Tobin, *American Jewish Philanthropy in the 1990s* (Waltham, Mass.: Maurice and Marilyn Cohen Center for Modern Jewish Studies/Institute for Community and Religion, Brandeis University, 1995), 34.

23. Lawrence N. Jones, "Serving the Least of These," *Foundation News* (1984), 25, 58-61.

24. Emmett D. Carson, "Patterns of Giving in Black Churches," in Robert Wuthnow, Virginia A. Hodgkinson, et al., *Faith and Philanthropy in America: Exploring the Role of Religion in America's Voluntary Sector* (San Francisco: Jossey-Bass, 1990), 249-250.

25. See Mordechai Rimor and Gary A. Tobin, "Jewish Giving Patterns to Jewish and Non-Jewish Philanthropy," in Robert Wuthnow, Virginia A. Hodgkinson, et al., *Faith and Philanthropy in America,* 134. See also Derek J. Penslar, "The Origins of Modern Jewish Philanthropy," in Warren F. Ilchman, Stanley N. Katz, and Edward L. Queen II, eds., *Philanthropy in the World's Traditions* (Bloomington, Ind.: Indiana University Press, 1998), 197-214.

26. Rimor and Tobin, "Jewish Giving Patterns," 145-147.

27. Anita H. Plotinsky, "From Generation to Generation: Transmitting the Jewish Philanthropic Tradition," in Charles H. Hamilton and Warren F. Ilchman, eds., *Cultures of Giving: How Region and Religion Influence Philanthropy* (San Francisco: Jossey-Bass, 1995), 117-131.

28. Walter Collier et al., *Financing African-American Churches: National*

*Survey on Church Giving* (Atlanta: Institute of Church Administration and Management, 1997), 1.

29. John Ronsvalle and Sylvia Ronsvalle, *Behind the Stained Glass Window: Money Dynamics in the Church* (Grand Rapids: Baker Books, 1996), 36, 52.

30. Kathryn Christenson, "Reframing Confirmation," *The Lutheran* (May 1999), 12-17.

**Chapter 3**

1. John Ronsvalle and Sylvia Ronsvalle, *Behind the Stained Glass Window: Money Dynamics in the Church* (Grand Rapids: Baker Books, 1996), 115-119.

2. Robert Wuthnow, *God and Mammon in America* (New York: Free Press, 1994), 139-140.

3. "Lutheran Brotherhood Reports: Charitable Giving to Churches" (Jan. 28, 2000).

4. Wuthnow, *God and Mammon in America*, 235.

5. Ronsvalle and Ronsvalle, *Behind the Stained Glass Window,* 330.

6. "Money and Congregational Life: A Group Discussion," *Reconstructionism Today* (winter 1999/2000), 7-9.

7. Arthur Waskow, *Down-to-Earth Judaism: Food, Money, Sex, and the Rest of Life* (New York: William Morrow, 1995), 219.

8. Robert Wuthnow, *Poor Richard's Principle: Recovering the American Dream Through the Moral Dimension of Work, Business, and Money* (Princeton, N.J.: Princeton University Press, 1996), 166.

9. "Would Jesus Drive a BMW? A Conversation with Tony Campolo," *Youthworker* (Spring 1994).

10. Wuthnow, *God and Mammon in America,* 151.

11. Some parallel concerns are being raised by some Jewish leaders about misuse of the term *tzedakah*. Rabbi Dennis Eisner of Hebrew Union College–Jewish Institute of Religion says he has to remind youth groups that holding a fundraiser to finance a youth trip is not *tzedakah*—which focuses on giving of one's own money or material possessions for the benefit of others.

12. Wuthnow, *God and Mammon in America,* 141-142, 144.

13. Loren B. Mead, *Financial Meltdown in the Mainline?* (Bethesda: Alban Institute, 1998), 87.

14. Anita H. Plotinsky, "From Generation to Generation: Transmitting the Jewish Philanthropic Tradition," in Charles H. Hamilton and Warren F. Ilchman, eds., *Cultures of Giving: How Region and Religion Influence Philanthropy* (San Francisco: Jossey-Bass, 1995), 117-131.

15. James Hudnut-Beumler, "Protestants and Giving: The Tithes that Bind?" in

Charles H. Hamilton and Warren F. Ilchman, eds., *Cultures of Giving: How Region and Religion Influence Philanthropy* (San Francisco: Jossey-Bass, 1995), 79-89.

16. "Would Jesus Drive a BMW?"

17. *Giving Better, Giving Smarter: Renewing Philanthropy in America* (Washington: National Commission on Philanthropy and Civic Renewal, 1997), 89.

18. Quoted in Ronsvalle and Ronsvalle, *Behind the Stained Glass Window*, 181.

19. Mead, *Financial Meltdown,* 119-120.

20. Mead, *Financial Meltdown,* 31.

21. Barry A. Kosmin, "New Directions in Contemporary Jewish Philanthropy: The Challenges of the 1990s," in Charles H. Hamilton and Warren F. Ilchman, *Cultures of Giving II: How Heritage, Gender, Wealth, and Values Influence Philanthropy* (San Francisco: Jossey-Bass, 1995), 41-51.

22. Some experts question whether the financial crisis is as serious as it is sometimes portrayed. Placing current financial patterns within a historical context, Mark Chavez speculates as to whether "much of the present sense of financial crisis . . . in American religion may be because of the inability to continue national programs and organizations that were overbuilt in a time of unusual plenty. . . . It may be helpful to extend our historical horizon so that the visual image of change regarding the financial health of American religion looks more like an inverted 'U' than a downward sloping straight line. That is, the twentieth-century story of national denominational organizations is not a story of linear decline but a story of a period of relative scarcity followed by a time of plenty followed by another period of relative scarcity." This hypothesis is offered in Mark Chavez, "Financing American Religion," in Mark Chavez and Sharon Miller, eds., *Financing American Religion* (Walnut Creek, Calif.: AltaMira, 1999), 180.

23. See, for example, Mead, *Financial Meltdown;* Ronsvalle and Ronsvalle, *Behind the Stained Glass Window;* Robert Wuthnow, *The Crisis in the Churches: Spiritual Malaise, Fiscal Woe* (New York: Oxford University Press, 1997); and Chavez and Miller, *Financing American Religion.*

24. Mead, *Financial Meltdown,* 82.

25. Mary J. Oates, *The Catholic Philanthropic Tradition in America* (Bloomington, Ind.: Indiana University Press, 1995), 168.

26. Daniel Conway, "Faith Versus Money: Conflicting Views of Stewardship and Fundraising in the Church," in Charles H. Hamilton and Warren F. Ilchman, eds., *Cultures of Giving: How Region and Religion Influence Philanthropy* (San Francisco: Jossey-Bass, 1995), 71-77.

27. The most comprehensive tools are from the Presbyterian Church (U.S.A.), the Evangelical Lutheran Church in America, and several dioceses of the Roman Catholic Church. Other resources are included in appendix A.

28. Robert Wuthnow, ed., *Rethinking Materialism: Perspectives on the Spiritual Dimension of Economic Behavior* (Grand Rapids: Eerdmans, 1995), 17.

29. Mead, *Financial Meltdown,* 103.

30. Eugene C. Roehlkepartain and Peter C. Scales, *Youth Development in Congregations: An Exploration of the Potential and Barriers* (Minneapolis: Search Institute, 1995), 49-51.

31. For overviews of many of the studies that have been conducted in recent years, see Chaves and Miller, eds., *Financing American Religion.*

32. Francis Edward Clark, *The Christian Endeavor Manual,* new and revised edition (Boston: United Society of Christian Endeavor, 1903, 1912), 11-13.

33. Clark, *Christian Endeavor Manual,* 184.

**Chapter 4**
1. Wirthlin Group, *The Prudential Spirit of Community Youth Survey: A Survey of High School Students on Community Involvement* (Newark: Prudential Insurance Company of America, 1995), 14, 16.

2. George H. Gallup, Jr., *The Spiritual Life of Young Americans: Approaching the Year 2000* (Princeton, N.J.: George H. Gallup International Institute, n.d.), 73.

3. Wirthlin Group, *Prudential Spirit,* 14, 16.

4. For a more detailed look at the historical trends in service and service-learning, see Richard J. Kraft, "Service-Learning: An Introduction to Its Theory, Practice, and Effects," *Education and Urban Society,* vol. 28, no. 2 (Feb. 1996), 131-159.

5. Robert Shumer and Charles C. Cook, *The Status of Service-Learning in the United States* (St. Paul, Minn.: National Service-Learning Clearinghouse, 1999).

6. Peter L. Benson et al., *A Fragile Foundation: Developmental Assets Among American Youth* (Minneapolis: Search Institute, 1999), 18.

7. Virginia A. Hodgkinson and Murray S. Weitzman, *Volunteering and Giving among Teenagers 12 to 17 Years of Age: Findings from a National Survey,* 1996 edition (Washington: Independent Sector, 1997), 21.

8. Lloyd D. Johnston, Jerald G. Bachman, and Patrick M. O'Malley, *Monitoring the Future: Questionnaire Responses from the Nation's High School Seniors, 1995* (Ann Arbor: Institute for Social Research, University of Michigan, 1997), 86.

9. Hodgkinson and Weitzman, *Volunteering and Giving Among Teenagers,* 1996 edition, 56.

10. Hodgkinson and Weitzman, *Volunteering and Giving Among Teenagers,* 1996 edition, 14, 30.

11. Lee M. Levison, "Choose Engagement Over Exposure," in Jane C. Kendall et al., *Combining Service and Learning: A Resource Book for Community and Public Service,* vol. 1 (Raleigh, N.C.: National Society for Experiential Education, 1990), 68-75.

12. Thomas Bright and John Roberto, "Introduction to Action and Service Programming," in Michael Moseley and John Roberto, *YouthWorks,* revised edition (Naugatuck, Conn.: Center for Ministry Development, 1996), section 11, part 2, p. 3.

13. Wirthlin Group, *Prudential Spirit,* 17.

14. Robert N. Bellah et al., *Habits of the Heart: Individualism and Commitment in American Life* (New York: Harper & Row, 1985).

15. Robert Wuthnow, *Acts of Compassion: Caring for Others and Helping Ourselves* (Princeton, N.J.: Princeton University Press, 1991), 17.

16. Ibid., 281.

17. See, for example, Alan S. Waterman, ed., *Service-Learning: Applications from the Research* (Mahwah, N.J.: Lawrence Erlbaum, 1997).

**Chapter 5**

1. There are, of course, many other valuable studies and approaches that add richness, balance, and nuance to those described here. Recent examples include Robert Wuthnow: *Elementary Kindness in an Age of Indifference* (New York: Oxford University Press, 1995); Robert Coles, *The Call of Service: A Witness to Idealism* (Boston: Houghton Mifflin, 1993); Richard J. Bentley and Luana G. Nissan, *The Roots of Giving and Serving* (Indianapolis: Indiana University Center on Philanthropy, 1996); Dean R. Hoge and Douglas L. Griffin, *Research on Factors Influencing Religious Giving* (Indianapolis: Ecumenical Center for Stewardship Studies, 1992); and Robert J. Chaskin and Teresa Hawley, *Youth and Caring: Developing a Field of Inquiry and Practice* (Chicago: Chapin Hall Center for Children at the University of Chicago, 1994).

2. Paul G. Schervish, "Gentle as Doves and Wise as Serpents: The Philosophy of Care and the Sociology of Transmission," in Schervish et al., *Care and Community in Modern Society: Passing on the Tradition of Service to Future Generations* (San Francisco: Jossey-Bass, 1995), 10. See also Paul G. Schervish et al., *Taking Giving Seriously* (Indianapolis: Indiana University Center on Philanthropy, 1993), 32-37.

3. Schervish, "Gentle as Doves and Wise as Serpents," 11.

4. Ibid., 12.

5. Ibid., 13.

6. Ibid., 14.

7. Ibid., 10-14. See also Paul G. Schervish et al., *Taking Giving Seriously* (Indianapolis: Indiana University Center on Philanthropy, 1993), 32-37.

8. Laurent A. Parks Daloz et al., *Common Fire: Lives of Commitment in a Complex World* (Boston: Beacon Press, 1996).

9. Summarized in Laurent Parks Daloz, *Can Generosity Be Taught?* (Indianapolis: Indiana University Center on Philanthropy, 1998).

10. At the time of writing, the most recent comprehensive reports available from this study were Virginia A. Hodgkinson and Murray S. Weitzman, *Giving and Volunteering in the United States: Findings from a National Survey,* 1996 edition (Washington: Independent Sector, 1996); and Virginia A. Hodgkinson and Murray S. Weitzman, *Volunteering and Giving among Teenagers 12 to 17 Years of Age: Findings from a National Survey,* 1996 edition (Washington: Independent Sector, 1997). Summary reports are available for more recent surveys, and updated information is available on Independent Sector's Web site: www.indepsec.org

11. Virginia A. Hodgkinson, "Key Factors Influencing Caring, Involvement, and Community," in Schervish et al., *Care and Community in Modern Society,* 21-50.

12. Ibid., 47.

13. Ibid., 48.

14. Ibid., 48-49.

15. Ibid., 49.

16. Hodgkinson and Weitzman, *Volunteering and Giving among Teenagers 12 to 17 Years of Age,* 32-35.

17. For more information on the developmental assets and their impact in young people's lives, see Peter L. Benson, et al., *A Fragile Foundation: The State of Developmental Assets among American Youth* (Minneapolis: Search Institute, 1999), and Peter C. Scales and Nancy Leffert, *Developmental Assets: A Synthesis of the Scientific Research on Adolescent Development* (Minneapolis: Search Institute, 1999).

18. Benson, et al., *A Fragile Foundation,* 90.

19. Peter L. Benson, "Religion, Religious Institutions, and the Development of Caring," unpublished paper presented at the Lilly Endowment Conference on Youth and Caring, Key Biscayne, Fla. (Feb. 26-27, 1992), 15.

20. Ibid., 16.

21. Based on analysis of surveys of young people in mainline Protestant congregations. No similar research is available on other traditions. However, Benson notes, "[I]t is likely that religious socialization in the Jewish tradition places relatively greater emphasis on defining, explaining, and commanding social justice, while within Christianity the accent is more on love, which tends to be translated into an interpersonal ethic rather than a social ethic" (33).

22. Benson, "Religion, Religious Institutions," 28.

23. Parks Daloz et al., *A Common Fire,* 17.

24. Readers familiar with Search Institute's work on developmental assets will recognize many of the themes in these culture shifts. Indeed, this focus on culture shifts builds on a similar framework in the foundational resource on developmental assets by Search Institute President Peter L. Benson, *All Kids Are Our Kids: What Communities Must Do to Raise Caring and Responsible Children and Adolescents* (San Francisco: Jossey-Bass, 1997), chapter 5.

25. Quoted in Peter L. Benson and Eugene C. Roehlkepartain, *Beyond Leaf Raking: Learning to Serve/Serving to Learn* (Nashville: Abingdon, 1993), 18.

26. Silvia Blitzer Golombek, "Children as Philanthropists: The Younger, the Better," in Schervish et al., *Care and Community in Modern Society*, 140, 143.

27. Diana Mendley Rauner, *They Still Pick Me Up When I Fall: The Role of Caring in Youth Development and Community Life* (New York: Columbia University Press, 2000).

28. In this case, we use "curriculum" in its colloquial sense, referring to the printed material developed and used to guide lessons or activities. We recognize that, in its true sense, the term "curriculum" encompasses the many elements that shape a learning experience, including interpersonal relationships and dynamics. See, for example, Maria Harris, *Fashion Me a People* (Louisville: Westminster John Knox, 1989).

29. *A Guide to Comprehensive Youth Programs: A Primer for Congregational Education and Action* (New York: Youth Division, Union of American Hebrew Congregations, 1997), 12.

30. Kenda Creasy Dean and Ron Foster, *The Godbearing Life: The Art of Soul Tending for Youth Ministry* (Nashville: Upper Room Books, 1998), 27.

31. Peter C. Scales et al., *The Attitudes and Needs of Religious Youth Workers: Perspectives from the Field* (Minneapolis: Search Institute, 1995), 10.

32. Dean and Foster, *The Godbearing Life,* 30.

33. From Eugene C. Roehlkepartain, *Building Assets in Congregations: A Practical Guide for Helping Youth Grow Up Healthy* (Minneapolis: Search Institute, 1998), 123.

34. National Conference of Catholic Bishops, *Renewing the Vision: A Framework for Catholic Youth Ministry* (Washington: U.S. Catholic Conference, 1997), 20-25.

35. Kenda Creasy Dean, "A Synthesis of the Research on, and a Descriptive Overview of Protestant, Catholic, and Jewish Religious Youth Programs in the United States," a working paper prepared for the Task Force on Youth Development and Community Programs, Carnegie Council on Adolescent Development (Feb. 1991), 112-113.

36. "Community Service Performed by High School Seniors," *National Center for Education Statistics and Educational Policy Issues: Statistical Perspectives* (Oct. 1995).

37. David Heffernan, *Service Opportunities for Youth* (Washington: Adolescent Pregnancy Clearinghouse, Children's Defense Fund, 1989), 5.

38. Thomas H. Groome, *Christian Religious Education: Sharing Our Story and Vision* (San Francisco: Harper & Row, 1980), 21.

39. For more on blending a reflection component into congregation-based youth service, see Peter L. Benson and Eugene C. Roehlkepartain, *Beyond Leaf Raking: Learning to Serve/Serving to Learn* (Nashville: Abingdon, 1993).

It includes a chapter blending service-learning approaches to reflection with Thomas Groome's "shared praxis" model of religious education.

40. Dale A. Blyth, Rebecca Saito, and Tom Berkas, "A Quantitative Study of the Impact of Service-Learning Programs," in Alan S. Waterman, ed., *Service-Learning: Applications from the Research* (Mahwah, N.J.: Lawrence Erlbaum, 1997), 51-52.

**Chapter 6**

1. A version of this framework was presented in Eugene C. Roehlkepartain, *Kids Have a Lot to Give: How Congregations Can Nurture Habits of Giving and Serving for the Common Good* (Minneapolis: Search Institute, 1999).

2. A comprehensive presentation of this approach is found in Peter L. Benson, *All Kids Are Our Kids: What Communities Must Do to Raise Caring and Responsible Children and Adolescents* (San Francisco: Jossey-Bass, 1997). An application of the approach to congregations can be found in Eugene C. Roehlkepartain, *Building Assets in Congregations: A Practical Guide for Helping Youth Grow Up Healthy* (Minneapolis: Search Institute, 1998).

3. Send your feedback to Gene Roehlkepartain, Search Institute, 700 S. Third St., Suite 210, Minneapolis, MN 55415; gener@search-institute.org

4. Warren F. llchman, Stanley N. Katz, and Edward L. Queen II, eds., *Philanthropy in the World's Traditions* (Bloomington, Ind.: Indiana University Press, 1998).

5. Elliott Abrams, "In the Temple of Philanthropy: American Jews Embrace a Civil Religion of Giving," *Philanthropy,* vol. 11, no. 3 (summer 1997), 10.

6. Carl S. Dudley and Sally A. Johnson, *Energizing the Congregation: Images that Shape Your Church's Ministry* (Louisville: Westminster John Knox, 1993), chapters 2-6. (The identifiers have been changed by the authors from "churches" to "congregations" to make the images more inclusive.)

7. Michael Lerner, *Jewish Renewal: A Path to Healing and Transformation* (New York: Grosset/Putnam, 1994), 304.

8. Mark Vincent, *Teaching a Christian View of Money: Celebrating God's Generosity* (Scottdale, Pa.: Herald Press, 1997), 20.

9. Some of Siegel's books of stories include: *Munbaz II and Other Mitzvah Heroes* (Pittsboro, N.C.: Town House Press, 1998); Good People (Pittsboro, N.C.: Town House Press, 1995); and *Heroes and Miracle Workers* (Pittsboro, N.C.: Town House Press, 1997).

10. Carl S. Dudley, *Civic Investing by Religious Institutions: How Churches Launch New Community Ministries* (Indianapolis: Indiana University Center on Philanthropy, 1997), 5-6. See also Carl S. Dudley, *Next Steps in Community Ministry* (Bethesda: Alban Institute, 1996).

11. Robert Wuthnow, *Acts of Compassion: Caring for Others and Helping Ourselves* (Princeton, N.J.: Princeton University, 1991), 254-55.

12. *Effective Christian Education: A National Study of Protestant Congregations—A Six-Denomination Report* (Minneapolis: Search Institute, 1990), 51.

13. Robert Wuthnow, *Growing Up Religious: Christians and Jews and Their Journeys of Faith* (Boston: Beacon Press, 1999), 98.

14. Secondary analysis of data reported in Peter L. Benson, Eugene C. Roehlkepartain, and I. Shelby Andress, *Congregations at Crossroads: A National Study of Adults and Youth in The Lutheran Church–Missouri Synod* (Minneapolis: Search Institute, 1995).

15. Eugene C. Roehlkepartain and Peter C. Scales, *Youth Development in Congregations: An Exploration of the Potential and Barriers* (Minneapolis: Search Institute, 1995), 49-51.

16. Virginia A. Hodgkinson and Murray S. Weitzman, *Volunteering and Giving among Teenagers 12 to 17 Years of Age: Findings from a National Survey,* 1996 edition (Washington: Independent Sector, 1997), 4.

17. *A Guide to Comprehensive Youth Programs: A Primer for Congregational Education and Action* (New York: Youth Division, Union of American Hebrew Congregations, 1997), 8.

18. See, for example, *A Guide to Comprehensive Youth Programs;* Michael Moseley and John Roberto, eds., *YouthWorks,* revised edition (Naugatuck, Conn.: Center for Ministry Development, 1996); Eugene C. Roehlkepartain, *Building Assets in Congregations;* and M. Steven Games, ed., *Lifegivers: A Practical Guide for Reaching Youth in a Challenging World* (Nashville: Abingdon, 1996); and Merton P. Strommen and Richard A. Hardel, *Passing On the Faith: A Radical New Model for Youth and Family Ministry* (Winona, Minn.: St. Mary's Press, 2000).

19. Robert Wuthnow, *Acts of Compassion: Caring for Others and Helping Ourselves* (Princeton, N.J.: Princeton University, 1991), 124.

20. Dean R. Hoge, "Explanations for Current Levels of Religious Giving," *New Directions for Philanthropic Fundraising,* 7 (spring 1995), 55.

21. Mordechai Rimor and Gary A. Tobin, "Jewish Giving Patterns to Jewish and Non-Jewish Philanthropy," in Robert Wuthnow, Virginia A. Hodgkinson, et al., *Faith and Philanthropy in America: Exploring the Role of Religion in America's Voluntary Sector* (San Francisco: Jossey-Bass, 1990), 135.

22. Peter L. Benson and Carolyn H. Eklin, *Effective Christian Education: A National Study of Protestant Congregations—A Summary Report on Faith, Loyalty, and Congregational Life* (Minneapolis: Search Institute, 1990), 38. See also Eugene C. Roehlkepartain, *The Teaching Church: Moving Christian Education to Center Stage* (Nashville: Abingdon, 1993).

23. Of the denominations represented in the Effective Christian Education study, the only one that appeared to maintain fairly steady levels of involvement from childhood through adolescence and into adulthood was the Southern Baptist Convention, which has a strong tradition of life-long learning. Among the Southern

Baptist congregations, roughly half of members in all age groups participated regularly in Christian education. However, among the five mainline denominations, which tend to place less emphasis on adult discipleship, the percentage of involvement dropped from 52 percent in grades seven through nine to 35 percent in grades ten through 12, and 28 percent among adults. See *Effective Christian Education: A Six-Denomination Report,* 53.

24. Susan Hogan, "All Saints Members Mind Treasures, Time in Living Out Parable of Talents," *Minneapolis Star Tribune* (June 21, 1997), B5, 8.

25. Mark Vincent, *Teaching a Christian View of Money: Celebrating God's Generosity* (Scottdale, Penn.: Herald Press, 1997), 31.

26. Anita H. Plotinsky, "From Generation to Generation: Transmitting the Jewish Philanthropic Tradition," in Charles H. Hamilton and Warren F. Ilchman, eds., *Cultures of Giving: How Region and Religion Influence Philanthropy* (San Francisco: Jossey-Bass, 1995), 122.

27. Alice H. Eagly and Shelly Chaiken, *The Psychology of Attitudes* (Orlando: Harcourt Brace & Company, 1993), 631.

28. Daniel Romer et al. "Social Influences on the Sexual Behavior of Youth at Risk for HIV Exposure," *American Journal of Public Health,* 84 (1994), 977-985; and Kathryn A. Urberg, Shiang-jeou Shyu, and Jersey Liang, "Peer Influence in Adolescent Cigarette Smoking," *Addictive Behaviors,* 15 (1990), 247-255.

**Chapter 7**

1. Craig Dykstra and Dorothy C. Bass, "Times of Yearning, Practices of Faith," in Dorothy C. Bass, ed., *Practicing Our Faith: A Way of Life for Searching People* (San Francisco: Jossey-Bass, 1997), 5.

2. See this initiative's Web site: www.syn2000.org

3. Arthur Waskow, *Down-to-Earth Judaism: Food, Money, Sex, and the Rest of Life* (New York: William Morrow, 1995), 6.

4. John Ronsvalle and Sylvia Ronsvalle, *At Ease: Discussing Money and Values in Small Groups* (Bethesda: Alban Institute, 1998).

5. Michael S. Hamilton, "More Money, More Ministry: The Financing of American Evangelicalism Since 1945," in Larry Eskridge and Mark A. Noll, eds., *More Money, More Ministry: Money and Evangelicals in Recent North American History* (Grand Rapids: Eerdmans, 2000).

6. This fund-raising approach was pioneered by the Heifer Project International, Box 8106, Little Rock, AR 72203; 800-422-0755; www.heifer.org. The organization provides detailed information for purchasing a gift animal or tree seedling to help families around the world become self-reliant.

7. Sharon Daloz Parks, "Household Economics," in Dorothy C. Bass, ed., *Practicing Our Faith: A Way of Life for Searching People* (San Francisco: Jossey-Bass, 1997), 56.

8. Robert Wuthnow, *Learning to Care: Elementary Kindness in an Age of Indifference* (New York: Oxford University Press, 1995), 38.

9. Robert Shumer. "Executive Summary: Describing Service-Learning: A Delphi Study" (St. Paul: University of Minnesota, 1993).

10. Peter C. Scales, "Does Service-Learning Make a Difference?" *Source Newsletter* (Jan. 1999), 2-3.

11. A practical guide to addressing each of these elements is Eugene C. Roehlkepartain, Tom Bright, and Beth Margolis-Rupp, *An Asset Builder's Guide to Service-Learning* (Minneapolis: Search Institute, 2000).

12. Jacqueline White, "Mexico Trip Puts Learning into Service," *Assets* (spring 2000), 10-11.

13. Lyn Baird, "Fanning the Flame," in Richard Kraft and James Kielsmeier, eds., *Experiential Education and the Schools* (Boulder, Colo.: Association for Experiential Education, 1986), 171.

14. From Peter L. Benson and Eugene C. Roehlkepartain, *Beyond Leaf Raking: Learning to Serve/Serving to Learn* (Nashville: Abingdon Press, 1993), 52.

15. Dan Conrad and Diane Hedin, *Youth Service: A Guidebook for Developing and Operating Effective Programs* (Washington: Independent Sector, 1987), 39.

16. See, for example, Harry Silcox, *A How-to Guide to Reflection: Adding Cognitive Learning to Community Service Programs* (Philadelphia: Brighton Press, 1993); *Reflection: The Key to Service Learning,* second edition (New York: National Helpers Network, 1998); James and Pamela Toole, "Reflection as a Tool for Turning Service Experience into Learning Experiences," in Carol W. Kinsley and Kate McPherson, eds., *Enriching the Curriculum Through Service-Learning* (Alexandria, Va.: Association for Supervision and Curriculum Development, 1995).

17. Based on David A. Kolb et al., *Organizational Psychology: An Experiential Approach* (Englewood Cliffs, N.J.: Prentice-Hall, 1979); and Glen L. Gish, "The Learning Cycle," in Jane C. Kendall et al., *Combining Service and Learning: A Resource Book for Community and Public Service,* vol. 2 (Raleigh, N.C.: National Society for Experiential Education, 1990), 198-205.

18. Kate McPherson, *Learning Through Service* (Mount Vernon, Wash.: Project Service Leadership, 1989).

19. See Benson and Roehlkepartain, *Beyond Leaf Raking,* chapter 7.

20. Adapted from Thomas H. Groome, *Christian Religious Education: Sharing Our Story and Our Vision* (San Francisco: Harper & Row, 1980), 208-23, and Thomas Groome, "Using Praxis in Your Classroom," *Youthworker Journal* (summer 1990), 20-26.

21. Diana Mendley Rauner, *They Still Pick Me Up When I Fall: The Role of Caring in Youth Development and Community Life* (New York: Columbia University Press, 2000), 52-53.

22. Humphrey Taylor, "When It Comes to Teaching Teens about Managing Money, Mothers Play a Bigger Role than Fathers," *Harris Poll #21* (Apr. 29, 1998).

23. Unpublished data from a sample of 99,462 6th- to 12th-grade youth in public and/or alternative schools who completed the *Search Institute Profiles of Student Life: Attitudes and Behaviors* survey during the 1996-97 school year. The sample includes surveys from 213 U.S. communities in 25 states. For more information, see Peter L. Benson et al., *A Fragile Foundation: The State of Developmental Assets Among American Youth* (Minneapolis: Search Institute, 1999). These findings are consistent with Independent Sector research showing that young people whose parents engage in volunteer work are more likely than other youth to do so themselves. See Virginia A. Hodgkinson and Murray S. Weitzman, *Volunteering and Giving among Teenagers 12 to 17 Years of Age: Findings from a National Survey,* 1996 edition (Washington: Independent Sector, 1997), 30.

24. See, for example, Chap Clark, *The Youth Worker's Handbook to Family Ministry* (Grand Rapids: Zondervan, 1997); Mark DeVries, *Family-Based Youth Ministry* (Downers Grove, Ill.: InterVarsity, 1994); Ben Freudenberg with Rick Lawrence, *The Family-Friendly Church* (Loveland, Colo.: Vital Ministry/Group Publishing, 1998); Diana Garland, *Family Ministry: A Comprehensive Guide* (Downers Grove, Ill.: InterVarsity Press, 1999); Leora W. Isaacs and Jeffrey Schein, *Targilon: A Workbook for Charting the Course of Jewish Family Education* (New York: Jewish Education Service of North America, 1996); *Learning Together: A Sourcebook on Jewish Family Education* (Denver: A.R.E. Publishing, 1987); Richard P. Olson and Joe H. Leonard Jr., *A New Day for Family Ministry* (Bethesda: Alban Institute, 1996); John Roberto, ed., *Family Works* (Naugatuck, Conn.: Center for Ministry Development, 1995); Eugene C. Roehlkepartain, *Building Assets in Congregations: A Practical Guide for Helping Youth Grow Up Healthy* (Minneapolis: Search Institute, 1998); Merton P. Strommen and Richard A. Hardel, *Passing on the Faith: A Radical New Model for Youth and Family Ministry* (Winona, Minn.: St. Mary's Press, 2000);

25. John Roberto, "The Center for Ministry Development: Promoting Innovative Ministry with Adolescents, Young Adults, and Families," *Family Ministry,* 13, 2 (summer 1999), 59-68.

26. Merton P. Strommen and Richard A. Hardel, *Passing on the Faith: A Radical New Model for Youth and Family Ministry* (Winona, Minn.: St. Mary's Press, 2000), 16-17.

27. Olson and Leonard, *A New Day for Family Ministry.*

28. Kathleen and James McGinnis, *Parenting for Peace and Justice: Ten Years Later* (Maryknoll, N.Y.: Orbis Books, 1990), 144.

29. Ibid, 95-96.

30. John Roberto, "Promoting Faith Development Today," in John Roberto, ed., *Family Works,* 15.

31. Ben Freudenberg with Rick Lawrence, *The Family-Friendly Church* (Loveland, Colo.: Vital Ministry/Group Publishing, 1998), 135

32. Freudenberg, ibid., 113.

33. Lutheran Brotherhood offers two workshops to support these kinds of conversations: "Parents, Kids, and Money," which focuses on elementary-age children; and "Parents, Teens, and Money," which focuses on middle- and high-school youth. Another innovative approach to engaging young people and parents together in study and learning in Christian churches is the "Total Family Sunday School" model from Faith Inkubators. This model involves weekly intergenerational, small-group study, followed by home study through the week. For information, write to Faith Inkubators, 1940 Greeley St., Suite 120, Stillwater, MN 55082, or visit the company's Web site: www.tfss.com

34. Eugene C. Roehlkepartain and Peter L. Benson, *Youth in Protestant Churches: A Special Search Institute Report* (Minneapolis: Search Institute, 1993), 125.

35. "Family Volunteering Creates Meaningful Holidays," press release from the Family Matters program of the Points of Light Foundation (Nov. 9, 1995).

36. Leif Kehrwald, "Families and Christian Practice," *Family Ministry,* 13, 4 (winter 1998), 48-58.

37. Unpublished data from a sample of 99,462 sixth- to 12th-grade youth. See note 23 above.

38. Cheryl Hall-Russell and Robert H. Kasberg, *African American Traditions of Giving and Serving: A Midwest Perspective* (Indianapolis: Indiana University Center on Philanthropy, 1997), 24.

39. Merton P. Strommen, *The Innovative Church: Seven Steps to Positive Change in Your Congregation* (Minneapolis: Augsburg Fortress, 1997). Another approach to congregational change is available in Gilbert R. Rendle, *Leading Change in the Congregation: Spiritual and Organizational Tools for Leaders* (Bethesda: Alban Institute, 1998). In addition, Synagogue 2000 was launched in 1997 with a focus on "the spiritual transformation of synagogue structure and culture." For information, visit its Web site at www.syn2000.org

40. Strommen, *The Innovative Church,* 78.

41. Ibid., 158.

42. For suggestions on connecting with other congregations around youth issues, see Ann Betz and Jolene L. Roehlkepartain, *Networking Congregations for Asset Building: A Tool Kit* (Minneapolis: Search Institute, 2001).

# $\mathcal{W}$elcome to the work of Alban Institute...
## the leading publisher and congregational
## resource organization for clergy and laity today.

Your purchase of this book means you have an interest in the kinds of information, research, consulting, networking opportunities and educational seminars that Alban Institute produces and provides. We are a non-denominational, non-profit 25-year-old membership organization dedicated to providing practical and useful support to religious congregations and those who participate in and lead them.

Alban is acknowledged as a pioneer in learning and teaching on *Conflict Management *Faith and Money *Congregational Growth and Change *Leadership Development *Mission and Planning *Clergy Recruitment and Training *Clergy Support, Self-Care and Transition *Spirituality and Faith Development *Congregational Security.

Our membership is comprised of over 8,000 clergy, lay leaders, congregations and institutions who benefit from:
❖ 15% discount on hundreds of Alban books
❖ $50 per-course tuition discount on education seminars
❖ Subscription to *Congregations*, the Alban journal (a $30 value)
❖ Access to Alban research and (soon) the "Members-Only" archival section of our web site www.alban.org

For more information on Alban membership or to be added to our catalog mailing list, call 1-800-486-1318, ext.243 or return this form.

Name and Title: _____

Congregation/Organization: _____

Address: _____

City: _____ Tel.: _____

State: _____ Zip: _____ Email: _____

BKIN

The Alban Institute
Attn: Membership Dept.
7315 Wisconsin Avenue
Suite 1250 West
Bethesda, MD 20814-3211